COMMODORE 64
EXPOSED

COMMODORE 64
EXPOSED

BRUCE BAYLEY

MELBOURNE HOUSE

Contributions by:
Andrew Paulomanolakos
Peter Falconer
Goodwin Yuen

Contents

Chapter 5

Chapter 6

Chapter 7

Appendices

CHAPTER 1

PROGRAMMING IN BASIC

BASIC is only one of the many languages used to communicate with computers. It is however, the most common language in the microcomputer world, so it's a good one to know. BASIC varies from computer to computer, but once one dialect is known it is easy to adapt to others. A knowledge of Commodore 64 BASIC is a solid basis for programming in BASIC on any computer.

COMMODORE 64 BASIC

Immediate and Program modes.

When the Commodore 64 is turned on it starts in immediate mode. In this mode, each line typed in and completed by pressing RETURN is executed immediately – hence the name.

Program mode is used to store programs. The name is something of a misnomer, but it is commonly used. Actually, you're still in immediate mode, but whenever BASIC sees a line that starts with a number, it executes the line by storing it in memory. The statements following the line number are executed only when you run the program.

e.g. typing   PRINT "HELLO" will cause HELLO to be displayed on the screen.

      typing   10 PRINT "HELLO" will cause that line to be stored in memory. There will be no display until you type RUN.

Points to note:

• Line numbers must be integers from 0 to 63999.

• Lines are sorted into numerical order no matter in what order they're typed.

• Typing a line number, then pressing RETURN deletes that line.

• Typing two lines with the same line number leaves only the second line in the program.

• Typing NEW deletes all program lines in memory so that you can type in a new program. If you don't do this the new program may have lines from the old program in it.

• To BASIC, a line can be up to 80 characters long (including the RETURN to terminate it) – ie. 2 screen rows. If you continue typing after this, none of the line will be stored in the program (if in program mode) or executed (if in immediate mode).

• You may put more than one statement on a line by seperating them with a colon.

e.g.   PRINT "H" : PRINT "E" : PRINT "L" : PRINT "L" : PRINT "O"

This can be done in both program and immediate modes.

1

- It is a good idea to start numbering lines at 100, and increasing at intervals of 10 or 20. This enables you to insert lines between existing lines.
- Although the BASIC interpreter stores any spaces you put in program lines, it ignores them when it executes. All spaces may therefore be omitted, although this makes programs difficult to read. The spaces are stored and when you list the program they are included in the listing. You cannot insert any spaces into keywords.

Control Structures

These are statements which control the order in which program lines are executed. BASIC has the simplest control structure — sequential execution — built in. In the absence of any other control structure, a program is executed from the lowest to the highest numbered line. If this were the only control structure available, programs would be very limited, so Commodore 64 BASIC has the following statements for program control. They allow your programs to make decisions, perform loops, and branch to different parts of the program.

IF – THEN

        IF [expression] THEN [statement(s)]
        e.g.   10 IF A=5 THEN B=A−1 : GOTO 200
                20 IF (A > 0 AND A < −3) THEN GOSUB 6000

If the expression is true then all statements following the THEN are executed. In line 10 above, for example, if A=5 then both statements B=A−1 and GOTO 200 are executed. If the expression is false, both statements are ignored, and the next line is executed.

The expression may be arithmetic, in which case the THEN statements are executed if the expression evaluates to any number other than 0. In other words, the Commodore 64 takes 0 to be FALSE and all else to be TRUE. This isn't particularly useful, and is bad programming style, since it isn't immediately obvious what is meant.

        e.g.   IF 5+6 THEN PRINT "YES"
                        result – prints YES
                IF A−5 THEN PRINT "YES"
                        result – doesn't print if A=5

If the expression evaluates to a string the result is unpredictable.

FOR – NEXT

        FOR [variable] = [start] TO [limit] STEP [step]
        [statement(s)]
        NEXT [variable]

e.g.

        10 FOR J=62 TO 70 STEP 1
        20 PRINT CHR$ (J) ; "IS ASCII" ; J
        30 NEXT J

2

This loops through lines 10-30 in the following way.
(i)   J is set to the start value - 62
(ii)   statements are executed until a NEXT statement appears
(iii)   the STEP factor is added to J. J = 63
(iv)   J is compared to the limit value - 70. If J is greater than 70 the loop is finished and execution proceeds from the line following the NEXT statement. If J is less than or equal to 70 the program loops back to line 20. If line 10 had been FOR J=70 TO 62 STEP −1 the values of J would be decremented by 1 every pass through the loop. When J is compared to the limit value 62 execution of the loop continues if J is greater than or equal to the limit value. Execution does not proceed to the line following the next statement until J is less than 62.
• The FOR variable must be a floating point variable
• [start], [limit] and [step] may be numeric variable names, expressions, negative, positive, integer or floating point.
• "STEP [step]" may be left out, in which case a STEP value of 1 is assumed. So in the example above "STEP 1" is not necessary.
• The variable name in the NEXT statement may be left out. In the example above, line 30 may read "30 NEXT"
• FOR loops are always executed at least once, even if the start value is initially greater than the limit for positive steps or less than the limit value for negative steps. This is because the comparison of the FOR variable with the limit is done at the end of the loop.
• If the step value is negative, the loop is terminated when the FOR variable is less than the limit. Again, the loop will be executed at least once.
• FOR statements may be nested to a maximum depth of 10. That is, you may have loops within loops.
e.g.

```
10 FOR J=1 TO 5
20 FOR K=1 TO 7
30 ...
40 FOR L=1 TO 3
50 ...
60 ...
70 NEXT L
80 NEXT K
90 NEXT J
```

When nesting loops be careful to terminate them correctly. The last FOR variable mentioned must be the first NEXT variable mentioned. If the variable names are left out of the NEXT statements, BASIC terminates the loops correctly. Each loop variable is placed on a stack. The NEXT statement takes the variable from the top. This is always the last one placed there. Hence the computer's "ability" to select the correct NEXT variable.

3

- There may be more than one variable name in a NEXT statement. The example above could have been terminated by 70 NEXT L,K,J. If you leave the variable names out BASIC will only terminate the last loop for you − ie. "70 NEXT" is only equivalent to "70 NEXT L".

GOTO

GOTO [line−number]

This is the simplest of the control statements. When executed, it causes the program to continue from the line number named. The unrestrained use of GOTOs can make programs difficult to follow, so it should be used with care.

- The line number must exist in the program.
- It cannot be a variable name or an arithmetic expression.

e.g.   10 X=50
        20 GOTO X − incorrect
        20 GOTO (40+30) −incorrect
        20 GOTO 200/10 - will goto line 200
        20 GOTO 200 − correct if line 200 exists

GOSUB

GOSUB [line−number] / RETURN

GOSUB is short for GO to SUBroutine. A subroutine is a collection of statements terminated by a RETURN statement.

When a GOSUB is executed, the program continues from the line number named, just like a GOTO. But, when the next RETURN statement is reached, the program returns to wherever the GOSUB is, continuing execution from the statement following the GOSUB.

e.g.   10   . . . .
        20   GOSUB 500 ⟶ 500   . . . .
        30   . . . . ⟵ 510   . . . .
        40   520   RETURN

The arrows indicate the path the program follows.

Subroutines are useful when there is a task which must be executed several times in the program. Using subroutines means you needn't write the same lines several times − you just GOSUB to them each time you need them.

- A RETURN statement without a GOSUB causes an error
- A RETURN statement is not written by pressing the RETURN key! They are quite different.
- There may be multiple RETURN statements in a subroutine.

e.g.   10 GOSUB 500

        ...

        500 IF X=5 THEN RETURN
        510 IF X=6 THEN B=X : RETURN
        520 C=X
        530 RETURN

This saves you having to jump to the end of the subroutine to a single RETURN

- Subroutines may be nested.

e.g.   10 GOSUB 520
```
       ...
       520 ...
       530 GOSUB 600
       540 ...
       550 RETURN
       ...
       600 ...
       610 GOSUB 700
       620 ...
       630 RETURN
```

BASIC does this by "stacking" the return addresses. When a GOSUB is reached, its address is put on a stack. At the next GOSUB its address is put on top of the first, and so on. When a RETURN is reached, the address on top of the stack is taken off, and the program branches to that address. At the next RETURN the address next on the stack is taken off, and so on. The addresses are stored in a special area called "stack", which is a fixed size (256 bytes). Therefore, by nesting too many GOSUBs you can run out of stack space. This will cause an "OUT OF MEMORY" error message to be displayed.

ON GOTO/GOSUB

e)   ON [variable] GOTO [line−number 1] , [line−number 2] ,...
     ON [variable] GOSUB [line−number 1] , [line−number 2] ,...

Depending on the value of the variable, the program will GOTO (or GOSUB) one of the line numbers. If the variable equals 1, the program will GOTO the first line number, if the variable equals 2, it will GOTO the second line number, and so on.

e.g.   ON X GOTO 200 , 60 , 60 , 75 , 500

- If the variable is 0 or greater than the number of line−numbers, the statement is ignored, and execution continues from the statement following the ON statement. If the variable is negative, it causes an error. If it is non-integer the fractional part is ignored and only the integer part is used.
- The variable may also be an arithmetic expression.

e.g.   ON (A * 3 + 4) GOSUB 100 , 1200 , 60
       ON (X−3*Y) GOTO 60 , 60 , 70 , 80 , 900

END

This statements stops the execution of a program. There may be several END statements in a program. This is handy for debugging (ie. getting rid of errors), since after an END has stopped the program, you may check the value of variables (by typing PRINT [variable]), change the value of variables, or look at the program listing (by typing LIST). You may then continue the program by typing CONT. However, CONT won't work if the program stopped on an error, or if you attempt to edit the program.

● It is not necessary to finish a program with an END statement.

DATA STRUCTURES

For a program to be useful it must be able to store information. It does this by using data structures. The following is a brief summary of the data structures available on the Commodore 64.

Bits and Bytes

A bit is the basic data structure used in all digital computers. The name is derived from Binary digIT, because a bit can take one of only two values, 1 or 0. Since it would be extremely cumbersome to store information bit by bit, there are more sophisticated data structures available to the programmer.

A byte is 8 bits. It can represent any number from 0 to 255 using the binary number system. The Commodore 64 is a byte addressable machine, which means that a byte is the smallest data structure which the programmer can directly examine or change — using PEEK and POKE.

(For more on bits, bytes and the binary number system see the section on Operators.)

Characters

Characters are stored as a code number in 1 byte. Thus there are potentially 256 character codes. The most common code is ASCII (for American Standard Code for Information Interchange). The Commodore 64 however, uses a slightly different code so as to cover colours and other special characters. Appendix A contains a table of ASCII and Commodore 64 character codes. You may also use CHR$ and ASC to explore Commodore 64 character codes.

e.g.   PRINT CHR$ (65) will print the character with code 65 — an "A"
       PRINT ASC ("B") will print the code for "B" — 66

● There is a difference between numeric characters and numbers. A number is read as a character when it appears between double quotes

e.g.   "5" — the character 5
       5 — the number 5

PRINT ASC ("5") will display the code for the character 5
PRINT ASC (5) won't work.

Variables

In general, when you store information you don't want to:
— decide where in memory to put it
— POKE it byte by byte into memory

— remember where you put it so you can retrieve it.

BASIC provides variables to do this for you. All you have to do is provide a name for your information. BASIC then attends to storage and retrieval of that information.

Rules for naming variables.

1) The first character must be a letter : A−Z, a−z
2) Except for the last character, the rest must be letters or numbers.
3) The last character must be −
    − "$" if you're storing strings
    − "%" if you're storing integers
    − a letter or a number if you're storing floating point numbers

e.g. AB$, NAME$ − string variables
     KI%, SKILL% − integer variables
     E2, TEMP − floating point variables

• Variable names can be any length.
• However, BASIC only recognises the first two characters plus the last one, if it's either "%" or "$".

e.g. NAME$ is seen as NA$
     NATURE$ is also seen as NA$
     TEMP is seen as TE
     SKILL% is seen as SK%

So don't use names like TEMP1 and TEMP2, since BASIC will treat them as one variable. Make sure different variable names differ in the first or second character.

• The advantage of long variable names is that they make programs easier to understand.
The disadvantage is that they take up more memory.
• Different variable types can have what appears to be the same name.

e.g. NA$, NA% and NA are all different variables.

• Variable names must not contain reserved words − ie. words which BASIC recognises as commands.

e.g. BASIC would read TOP$ as TO P$ since TO is a reserved word. This is a consequence of spaces between keywords and variables being optional.

FIRSTHENS would be read as FIRS THEN S since THEN is a reserved word.

This type of thing usually results in a SYNTAX ERROR in lines that look OK.

• Assigning values to variables is done using "="

e.g. NAME$ =   "JOHN"
     SKILL%   =   50
     FROD$ =   NAME$ — this assigns the value of
                                    NAME$ to FROD$

SKILL% = SKILL% + 10 — this takes the old value of SKILL%, adds 10, and assigns the result as the new value of SKILL%

- As the name implies, the value of variables may vary.
- Only the correct type of information may be assigned to a variable.

Trying to assign a number to a string variable, or a string to a numeric variable will cause a TYPE MISMATCH error.

e.g. NAME$ = 72 — type mismatch
SKILL% = "HARRY" — type mismatch

String Variables

A string is a series of characters contained within opening and closing quotes.

e.g. "This is a string"
Thisisnotastringitisaverylongvariablename

- Strings can be concatenated — ie. joined together using the "+" symbol

e.g. B$ = "THE COMMO "
A$ = B$ + "DORE 64"

The value of A$ is now the string "THE COMMODORE 64"

- Concatenation can be used to put characters in strings that you couldn't normally put in — for example, the double quote character.

e.g. A$ = " "STRING" " will not work because it will be read as an empty string (" "), then STRING, then another empty string. This will not make sense to BASIC

A$ = CHR$ (34) + "STRING" + CHR$ (34)

This concatenates the value of CHR$ (34), ", with STRING and, ", giving "STRING"

This technique can also be used to give multicoloured displays

e.g. A$ = CHR$ (30) +"THE" + CHR$ (31) + "END"
PRINT A$ will now display a green THE and a blue END.

- String variables can be very useful in getting "bombproof" input from the keyboard.

For example, imagine you are writing a program which at some point prompts the user to type in a number. You can do this by using
INPUT "NUMBER",A

To execute this the Commodore 64 prints the string and a question mark, and waits for the user to type in a number which it will assign as the value of A. But, if the user types in a non−numeric character, this will cause the error message REDO FROM START to be displayed. It skips down a line and displays the question mark again, waiting for a number. It will continue to do this until a number is input, or the program is stopped. This can be confusing to a user who doesn't know the meaning of REDO FROM START, and it can also destroy screen displays.

8

To avoid this, use

    INPUT "NUMBER",A$

Now the Commodore 64 expects a string, so whatever(almost) the user types will be OK. Of course this means that the program will have to do a little more work, converting the string to a number. To do this, use

    A=VAL(A$)

If A$ is a string containing only a number, A will become that number

e.g. A$ = "7.63"

    A = VAL (A$)

The value of A is now 7.63

If A$ contains non−numeric characters, VAL(A$) will return 0. Thus, the programmer can arrange to print meaningful error messages and reprompt the user without destroying screen displays.

• Commodore 64 BASIC has extensive string manipulation functions − RIGHT$, LEFT$, MID$, + (see Commodore 64 BASIC Commands)

• If no value is given to a string variable, its value is the empty string.

Floating Point Variables

Floating point numbers can be integers, fractions preceded by a decimal point, or a combination of the two.

e.g. 6, 7.346, 0.593, −0.762, −3

• They can be up to 9 digits long

• If a number with 10 or more digits is entered, it is automatically converted to scientific notation.

e.g. 12345678912

    is displayed as -

    1.23456789E+10

The number after the E indicates the number of positions the decimal point must be moved to give its true position. If it is positive, the decimal point is shifted to the right; if negative, to the left.

Note that the last two digits in the original number are rounded off. In general, if the 10th digit is 5 or more, the number is rounded up. If it is 4 or less, it is rounded down.

e.g. 1234567886 is displayed as 1.23456789E+9

    .1000000014 is displayed as .100000001

• There is a limit to the size of the numbers the Commodore 64 can handle

    smallest > 2.93873588E−39

    largest < 1.70141183E+38

Any number smaller than the lower limit is treated as 0. Any number larger than the upper limit gives an OVERFLOW ERROR.

• Floating point numbers can be entered from the keyboard in scientific notation.

• Floating point variables don't have a special last character

e.g. FP, FLOAT, X, L1

- If no value is given to a floating point variable, its value is 0

Integer Variables

Integers are numbers without a decimal point. They may be negative or positive. Unsigned integers are assumed to be positive.

e.g.   6, +63, −7, −7934621
- Integer variables are distinguished by % as the last character.
e.g.   NUM%, SC%, F%
- Integers may be assigned to floating point variables since they are a subset of floating point numbers. However, they will take 5 bytes for storage compared to 2 bytes if assigned to integer variables.
- If no value is given to an integer variable its value is 0.
- In most calculations the Commodore 64 converts integers to floating point numbers and, if necessary, converts the result back to an integer. It is therefore slower to use integer variables than to use floating point variables.

Arrays

Arrays are used to store large amounts of related information without having to assign a variable name to each data item. Instead, a name is assigned to the array as a whole, and the individual data items are referred to by their position in the array.
- Arrays are set up using a DIM statement

e.g.   DIM A$ (12)
This will set up a 1 dimensional string array with 13 elements. There are 13 because numbering of array elements starts from 0. This array has the elements A$ (0) through to A$ (12).
       DIM B% (4)
This sets up an integer array of 5 elements − B% (0) to B% (4)
       DIM C (2,4)
This sets up a 2 dimensional floating point array with 15 elements, 3 rows each of 5 elements.

C (0,0)	C (0,1)	C (0,2)	C (0,3)	C (0,4)
C (1,0)	C (1,1)	C (1,2)	C (1,3)	C (1,4)
C (2,0)	C (2,1)	C (2,2)	C (2,3)	C (2,4)

       DIM D$ (1,1,1)
This sets up a 3 dimensional string array of 8 elements − D$ (0,0,0) to D$ (1,1,1)
- Array elements are used just as a variable of the same type is.
e.g.   PRINT C (1,3)
       X=C (2,1)
       D$ (1,0,1)="HI"

- You cannot refer to the entire array at one time.
e.g. "PRINT A$" will not display the 13 elements of the array A$. To do this you would need the following:
FOR J=0 TO 12 : PRINT A$ (J) : NEXT
- Arrays can hold only one type of data. An attempt to store an integer in a string array, or a string in a floating point array will produce a TYPE MISMATCH error.
- Like variables, array elements have default values. When an array is first DIMensioned, all its elements take the default value for that variable type. ie. a string array is filled with null strings, a numeric array is filled with 0's.
- Arrays can also have default sizes. That is, you can refer to an array element without having first DIMensioned the array. However, this only applies to 1 or 2 dimensional arrays. The default DIMension is 10 – ie. 11 elements for each subscript used to reference an array element. In this case the Commodore 64 has implicitly DIMensioned the array for you. This can be confusing when the program is read later, so it's better to explicitly DIMension all arrays – ie. use a DIM statement.
- Arrays can be DIMensioned only once in a program. This also applies to arrays the Commodore 64 has implicitly DIMensioned for you. In other words,
10 LET A (1) = 0
20 DIM A (5)
will result in a RE–DIMENSIONED ARRAY error

Operators

Expressions are made up of operators and operands. Operators are symbols recognized by the Commodore 64 as representing operations to be performed on the operands. Operands may be variables, constants or other expressions. Expressions return a value, and hence may be used almost anywhere a variable of the same type could be used. There are exceptions to this however, such as GOTO statements. These exceptions are explicitly noted in the description of BASIC commands.

Arithmetic Operators

Arithmetic expressions return an integer value if all operands are integers, and a floating point value if any of the operands are floating point numbers. Most of these operators you will have met before, so a few examples will suffice.

Addition '+'
6+4, B%+C+6

Subtraction '−'
7−3, 18−36, B%−C
The minus sign is also used to signify a negative number.

Multiplication '*'
7*3, B%*8, 16*C*B%

Division '/'
The value on the left of the slash is divided by the value on the right.
7/4, B%/C

Exponentiation '↑'
The value on the left of the arrow is raised to the power of the value on the right.
A↑5, 2↑3, 6↑B%

Order of evaluation
An expression may contain multiple operators. The order of evaluation of the sub–expressions depends on the precedence of the operator in each sub–expression. Operators with the highest precedence are carried out first. A table of operator precedences appears at the end of the section on operators.

String Operators

Concatenation '+'
The plus sign can also be used to concatenate strings.
e.g. "FREE" + "DOM" returns "FREEDOM".
     if A$="STING" and B$="RAY"
     A$+B$ returns "STINGRAY"
Concatenation can be used to build strings up to 255 characters long. An attempt to build a longer string will result in a STRING TOO LONG error.

Relational Operators

These are used to compare strings or numbers. If the expression is true, −1 is returned, if false, 0 is returned. This means that it is possible to perform arithmetic operations on the result of a relational expression. The operators are:

'='	: equals
'>'	: is greater than
'<'	: is less than
'=<' or '<='	: is less than or equal to
'=>' or '>='	: is greater than or equal to
'<>'	: not equal to

e.g. 6 = 6 - returns true (−1)
     6 < 4 - returns false (0)
     6 < 6 - returns 0
     6 <=6 - returns −1
     A% < > B% - result depends on the value of A%, B%
Strings can also be compared. This is done character by character, using the Commodore 64 character code.

e.g. "C" < "D" returns true (−1) since the code for 'C' −67− is less
than the code for 'D' −68
"CAT" > "CATION" results in false (0)
A$=C$+D$ result depends on the values of A$, C$ and D$

Boolean Operators

These, named after the logician George Boole, are used to carry out
logical operations.

AND

The result of an AND expression is true only if both operands are true,
false otherwise.
e.g. 6 > 5 AND 4 < 5 returns true
6 < 5 AND 4 < 5 returns false
6 > 5 AND 5 < 4 returns false
IF A=22 AND B=20 GOTO 600 − result: GOTO line 600 if both A=22
and B=20

OR

The result of an OR expression is true if either operand is true, false only
if both operands are false.
e.g. 6 > 5 OR 4 < 5 returns true
6 < 5 OR 4 < 5 returns true
6 < 5 OR 5 < 4 returns false
IF A=22 OR B=20 OR C=6 THEN GOSUB 20 − result: GOSUB 20 if
any of the conditions are true

NOT

This takes only one operand. The result is the logical opposite of the
operand.
e.g. NOT (6 > 5) returns false
(6 < 5 OR 4 < 5) returns false
A single operand can be tested for true or false. It acts as if it has ' < > 0'
appearing after it, so any value other than 0 will return true.
e.g. IF 6 THEN GOTO 60 − result: GOTO executed
IF AHIT% THEN GOSUB 700 - result: depends on the value of the
variable AHIT%
Boolean operations can also be carried out on bits. However, this is best
described after a more detailed discussion of the binary number system.

Table of Operator Precedences

Precedence	Operator	Meaning
9	()	Used to over-ride normal precedences
8	'	exponentiation
7	—	signifies negative number
6	*	multiplication
6	/	division
5	+	addition, concatenation
5	—	subtraction
4	=	equals
4	< >	not equal to
4	<	less than
4	>	greater than
4	< = or = <	less than or equal to
4	> = or = >	greater than or equal to
3	NOT	logical opposite
2	AND	logical AND
1	OR	logical inclusive OR

• As noted above, parentheses, (), can be used to over-ride precedences. You can, for example, force an addition to be carried out before a multiplication by parenthesising the addition expression.

e.g. 4*6+2 returns 26

4*(6+2) returns 32

Operators with the same precedence are executed from left to right.

BINARY AND HEXADECIMAL NUMBER SYSTEMS

The decimal, binary and hexadecimal number systems all use the same principle. Each digit position in a number represents the power to which the base is raised. The digit in a position is multiplied by the result of the base being raised to its relevant power, and the results of these calculations are added to give the final value. The only difference between the three number systems is the base. The decimal system uses 10, the binary system 2 and the hex system 16.

e.g. decimal

$$\begin{array}{ccc} 1 & 2 & 4 \\ 10^2 & 10^1 & 10^0 \end{array}$$

$$= 100 + 20 + 4 = 124$$

binary

$$\begin{array}{cccccc} 1 & 0 & 1 & 1 & 0 & 1 \\ 2^5 & 2^4 & 2^3 & 2^2 & 2^1 & 2^0 \end{array}$$

decimal equivalent $= 32 + 0 + 8 + 4 + 0 + 1 = 45$

When working with hex, the letters A − F are used as the hex equivalents of the decimal numbers 10 — 15

e.g.

$$\begin{array}{cc} F & 3 \\ 16^1 & 16^0 \end{array}$$

decimal equivalent $= 240 + 3 = 243$

When addresses need to be POKEd into memory (as for the USR function) they must be POKEd a byte at a time even though they are 2 bytes long. To calculate the decimal POKE values for each of the two bytes, convert the number into hex, then change the two hexadecimal bytes back to decimal.

e.g. hex address 1D00

In decimal this is 7424, but you can't POKE this value. So take the high byte (1D) and convert it to decimal

$$\begin{array}{cc} 1 & D \\ 16^1 & 16^0 \end{array}$$

$$= 16 + 13 = 29 \qquad \text{POKE Address} + 1, 29$$

now the low byte

$$\begin{array}{cc} 0 & 0 \\ 16 & 16^0 \\ 0 & 0 = 0 \end{array} \qquad \text{POKE Address, 0}$$

Logical Operations on Bits

When AND, OR and NOT operands have numeric operands they are first converted to 2 byte 2's complement integers in the range -32768 to 32767. If they are not in this range an error message results.

The logical operation is then carried out on bits. If the operator is AND (or OR) the zero bit of operand 1 is ANDed (or ORed) with the zero bit of operand 2. This is repeated for the bit 1 pair, the bit 2 pair and so on.

e.g.

$$\begin{array}{cc} 1 & 1 \\ \underline{\text{AND } 1} & \underline{\text{AND } 0} \\ = 1 & = 0 \end{array}$$

ORing two bits which both have value 0 results in a 0. Any other combination produces 1.

e.g.   0   1

     OR $\underline{0}$ OR $\underline{0}$

      =0   =1

If the operator is NOT, all of the bits are complemented, i.e. a 1 becomes a 0 and vice versa.

Masks

As you will see it is sometimes necessary to change or read the values of only some bits of a byte, leaving the others unchanged or unread. The method used to do this is called masking.

For example, to check the value of only the last 4 bits of byte 36876 we AND the mask 15 with the byte value. It's easier to see how this works in binary notation.

```
value of 36876   – – – – 1 0 1 0
AND 15           0 0 0 0 1 1 1 1
                =0 0 0 0 1 0 1 0
```

Because the first 4 bits of the mask are 0, ANDing them will always produce 0 in the first 4 bits of the result, no matter what values were in the first 4 bits of 36876. Because the last 4 bits of the mask are 1, ANDing them will leave the values of the last 4 bits of 36876 unchanged. In general, to make a mask for PEEKing, put a 1 in bit positions you want unchanged, a 0 in those you don't want to know about.

For POKEing 1 into certain bits, an OR mask should be used. For example, to set bit 2 in 36876 OR the mask 4.

e.g. POKE 36876, PEEK(36876) OR 4

Again, it's easier to see how this works in binary.

```
value of 36876   – – – – 1 0 1 0
OR 4             0 0 0 0 0 1 0 0
=                – – – – 1 1 1 0
```

To POKE 0 into certain bits, AND a mask with 0 bits in the positions you want set to 0, 1 in those you want left unchanged.

CHAPTER 2

COMMODORE 64 BASIC Commands

The following describes, in alphabetic order, all the BASIC commands available on the Commodore 64. Those that are described as functions return values, like expressions, and can therefore be used where values of the appropriate type can be used. As with expressions, there are exceptions to this. Note that functions appearing in expressions are evaluated before operators, unless the operators are parenthesized.

ABS

: function
: ABS ([number])
ABS ([numeric variable])
ABS ([numeric expression])
: returns the absolute value of its argument ie. positive values are unchanged, negative values become their positive equivalents
e.g. ABS (6) returns 6
ABS (−72.3) returns 72.3
ABS (6+4*−3) returns 6
ABS (A%) returns positive magnitude of A%

AND

: operator
: [expression] AND [expression]
: returns true (−1) if both expressions are true
returns false (0) if either or both expressions are false
e.g. IF X=1 AND Y < =7 THEN GOTO 60
IF HIT% AND Z < > 6 THEN GOSUB 70
NOTE: AND can also operate on other numeric values
(see page 15).

ASC

: function
: ASC ([character string])
ASC ([string variable])
: returns the character code value of the first character in the string
e.g. ASC (A) returns 65
ASC (BAT) returns 66
ASC (A$) returns code of first character of A$
ASC ("") null string produces ILLEGAL QUANTITY error

17

ATN

    : function
    : ATN ([number])
     ATN ([numeric expression])
    : returns the arctangent of its argument in radians. The result is in
     the range: $+\sqrt{2}$ to $-\sqrt{2}$
     e.g. ATN (3) returns 1.24904577
          ATN (6*3−15) returns 1.24904577

CHR$

    : function
    : CHR$ ([number])
     CHR$ ([numeric expression])
     The argument to CHR$ must be between 0 and 255.
    : returns the single character string whose code is equal to the
     CHR$ argument
     e.g. CHR$ (65) returns 'A'
          PRINT CHR$(13) will print a RETURN − ie. the cursor will
          act as though the RETURN key has been pressed.
          Colour and reverse mode can also be controlled in this way.

CLOSE

    : statement
    : CLOSE [file−number]
    : closes the file started in an OPEN statement. You should execute
     a PRINT# to that file before closing it, to make sure that all data
     has been transmitted from the buffer.
     e.g. OPEN 1,4 :PRINT#1, END DATA : CLOSE 1

CLR

    : statement
    : CLR
    : This is not equivalent to the CLR key! This statement clears out
     any variables that have been defined, un−DIMensions any arrays
     that have been defined and RESTORES the DATA pointer to the
     beginning of data. It also closes all logical files currently open. The
     commands RUN, LOAD and NEW all automatically execute a
     CLR statement. Note that the program itself is left untouched after
     a CLR statement.
     e.g. 10 A% = 53 : CLR : PRINT A%
          This will display a 0

CMD

    : statement
    : CMD [file-number]
     Normally, the screen is used to display output - i.e. it is the default

output device. The CMD statement changes the default output device to the file number given as argument. This enables you to redirect everything normally displayed by the Commodore 64 to, for example, the printer. A CMD statement must be preceded by an OPEN statement. There are 3 ways to exit the CMD mode:

1) Press RUN/STOP and RESTORE keys. This will reset the Commodore 64 to its default condition.

2) Use the CMD statement to change the default output. e.g. CMD 3 makes the screen the default.

3) Execute a PRINT# [file−number]. This is preferred since it also empties the printer buffer.

e.g. 10 OPEN 1,4 - opens a channel to the printer
      20 CMD 1 - makes printer default output
      30 LIST - lists the program currently in memory to the printer
      40 PRINT#1 - makes sure the printer buffer is empty, and exits the CMD mode
      50 CLOSE 1 - closes the channel to the printer

CONT

: statement

: CONT

: This continues a program which has stopped due to a STOP keypress, or the execution of a STOP or END statement within a program. CONT will not work if the program stopped due to an error, or if an error is made while the program is stopped, or if any attempt is made to edit the program (even if nothing in the program is actually changed). Variable values may be examined and changed, and the program may be listed.

COS

: function

: COS ([numeric expression or variable or constant])

: returns the cosine of the argument in radians

   e.g. COS (0.4) returns 0.921060994

DATA

: statement

: DATA [constant], [constant],...,...,...

There may be one or more numeric or string constants. String constants need not appear within double quotes, unless the string contains graphics characters, commas, spaces or colons. Two commas with nothing between them will be read as either 0 or the null string, depending on the variable type the data is being read into . DATA statements may appear anywhere in a program. Since they need not be explicitly executed during the running of the program they may appear after an END statement.

19

: Provides data for a READ statement

    e.g. 10 DATA 6, −73.2, HELLO,"10 DATA", "A.,B"

           20 DATA 7,23,,GOODBYE

: Note: DATA statements cannot be used in immediate mode.

DEF FN

: statement

: DEF FN [name] ([parameter]) = [expressions]

[name] must be a floating point variable name 5 characters or less in length. [parameter] must be a numeric variable name. [expression] must be numeric, user–defined; string functions are illegal. Previously defined functions may appear in [expression]

: defines a function with 1 parameter which may be referenced later in the program

    e.g. 10 DEF FNA (X) = X ꜛ 3 - define the function

          20 PRINT FNA (2) - execute the function, replacing the parameter with value 2 result - displays 8 (2 ꜛ 3)

          30 PRINT FNA (Z) - replace parameter with value of Z result - displays value of Z ꜛ 3

: Note: Can only be used in program mode, although functions defined in program mode may be used in immediate mode.

DIM

: statement

: DIM[variable] ([integer],[integer],...)

: The [variable] identifies the array name and type. The integers indicate the number of elements in each dimension of the array. Since numbering of array elements starts from 0, DIM A(10) defines an array with 11 elements. The number of integers indicates the number of dimensions in the array. DIM A$(4,4) defines a 2 dimensional array of 25 elements. A DIM statement may define more than one array.

    e.g. DIM A$ (6), B (7,2), C% (1,2)

: defines an array. One or two dimensional arrays of 11 elements (1 per dimension) may be used without a DIM statement, since the Commodore 64 will implicitly define them for you when they are first referenced.

Arrays may be DIMensioned only once (even those implicitly defined).

Only elements of the type specified by the array name may be stored in the array.

The following table can be used to calculate the amount of memory used by arrays:

5 bytes — array name

2 bytes — each dimension

2 bytes/element — each integer value

5 bytes/element — each floating point value
3 bytes — each string variable
1 byte/character — in each string element
e.g. 10 DIM A$ (10) - defines string array of 11 elements
     20 DIM B% (3,5) - 2 dimensional integer array of 24 elements
     30 DIM C$ (6) , D (7,6,3) - string array - 7 elements and floating point array — 224 elements
     40 PRINT C$ (3) - displays fourth element of array C$
     50 D (1,4,2) = 6.2 - assigns 6.2 as value of D (1,4,2)
     60 A$ = C$ (1) - assigns value of C$ (1) to A$
(See Data Structures section for details of arrays)

END

: statement
: END
: stops a program and returns control to the user. Doesn't clear variables, array pointers or program, so CONT may be used to continue the program. There may be any number of END statements in a program. Useful for debugging.
e.g. 100 INPUT "CONTINUE", A$
     110 IF A$ = "NO" THEN END
     —
     —
     —
     200 END

EXP

: function
: EXP ([number])
: returns e (2.71828183) raised to the power of [number]
: e.g. EXP (2) returns 7.38905613
:

FOR-TO-STEP- / NEXT

: statement
: FOR[variable] = [start] TO [limit] STEP [step] / NEXT [variable]
  FOR [variable] = [start] TO [limit] / NEXT [variable]
  FOR [variable] = [start] TO [limit] / NEXT
  [variable] must be floating point. When STEP is omitted [step] is assumed to be 1. [start], [limit] and [step] may be negative, positive, constants, variables or expressions
: performs a loop through all statements between the FOR and NEXT statements.

21

A FOR loop is always executed at least once, since the variable value is compared to the limit at the end of the loop.

The loop terminates when the variable value is greater than the limit (if [step] is positive) or less than the limit (if [step] is negative). FOR loops may be nested to a depth of 10. When nested loops terminate at the same point the NEXT statement may contain more than one variable name. e.g. NEXT I,J,K. In such a case make sure the order is correct. Innermost loops must terminate first.

```
e.g.  10 FOR J = 7 TO B STEP −3
      20 ...
      30 ...
      40 NEXT J

      10 FOR J = 0 TO 6
      20 ...
      30 FOR K = 0 TO −5 STEP −1
      40 ...
      50 ...
      60 NEXT K, J
```

Note: When used in immediate mode, a multiple statement line is necessary.

```
FOR J = 1 TO 5 : PRINT CHR$ (J) : NEXT
```

FRE

: function
: FRE ([dummy value]) - the value of dummy is unimportant.
: returns the number of free bytes of memory, as is done automatically when the Commodore 64 is started. If the result returned is negative, add 65536 to get the true number of free bytes. FRE(0) — (FRE(0) < 0) * 65536 will always return the correct value
e.g. PRINT FRE (0)

GET

: statement
: GET [variable]
: checks the keyboard buffer and assigns the first character in it to the variable. If there is nothing in the buffer it assigns the null string to a string variable, or 0 to a numeric variable. The character it GETs is not echoed on the screen. A RETURN keypress is not necessary after typing the character. In fact it will GET a RETURN quite happily, just as it would almost any other character. Since GET doesn't wait for a key to be pressed, it is usually placed in a loop.

e.g. 10 GET A$: IF A$ = " " THEN GOTO 10
     5 PRINT "PASSWORD ?"
     20 GET P$
     30 IF P$ = " " THEN 20 − wait for keypress
     40 IF P$ = CHR$(13) THEN END − check for RETURN to
     signal end of password
     50 PW$ = PW$ + P$ − build password, character by
     character in PW$. Note that PW$ starts off as " ", the null
     string.
     60 GOTO 20 − get next character of password
     Note: GET cannot be used in immediate mode.

GET#

: statement
: GET# [file−number],[variable]
: same as GET, but gets characters from a previously OPENed
  input device such as cassette or disk drive.
  e.g. 10 OPEN 1,3
       20 FOR J = 1 TO 30
       30 GET#1,B$: A$ = A$ + B$
       40 NEXT
       50 CLOSE 1
This gets a buffer full of data from input device, stops device and
then proceeds to read the data from the buffer. In this case it gets
the first 30 character from the buffer and builds up the string A$
character by character.

GOSUB/RETURN

: :statement
: :GOSUB[line−number] / RETURN
  [line−number] cannot be a variable or expression
: branches to [line−number]. Execution continues from this line
  until a RETURN statement is read. Then control branches back to
  the GOSUB statement. Execution continues from the statement
  after theGOSUB statement.
  There may be more than one RETURN statement to cause the
  branch back to GOSUB. If a RETURN statement is read without a
  GOSUB first having been executed a RETURN WITHOUT
  GOSUB error will result. GOSUBs may be nested.
  Note: The RETURN statement and the RETURN key are quite
  different.
: e.g.   10 GOSUB 560
       ...
       560 IF K$ = "Y" THEN GOSUB 600 : RETURN
       570 IF K$ = "N" THEN PRINT "WHY NOT" : RETURN

580 PRINT "ANSWER MUST BY Y OR N"
590 RETURN

...

600 ...

...

675 RETURN

This example shows the use of multiple RETURNs and nesting of GOSUBs. GOSUB 600 is nested inside subroutine 560. GOSUBs may be nested to a greater depth if desired.

(For more on GOSUB see Control Structure section)

GOTO

: statement
: GOTO [line−number]
   [line−number] cannot be a variable or expression.
: causes the program to branch to [line-number] if such a line exists. It is also used in immediate mode to start a program from a particular line, (same as RUN).
   e.g. 10 GOTO 200

   ...
   200 ... − execution continues here

IF − THEN

: statement
: IF [condition] THEN [statement(s)]
   [condition] may be logical expression, numeric expression or variable name.
: If the condition is true the statements after the THEN are executed. If the condition is false the THEN statements are ignored and execution continues from the next line.
   Logical expression evaluate to −1 (true) or 0 (false). Numeric expressions and variables are treated as false if they evaluate to 0 and as true if they evaluate to any other value.
   When the statement immediately following the THEN is a GOTO [line−number], the line−number alone is sufficient.
   e.g. IF A$ = "YES" THEN 70 will execute a GOTO 70 if the condition is true.
   Alternatively, THEN may be omitted if GOTO is retained.
   e.g. IF A$ = "YES" GOTO 70
   e.g. 10 IF (A = 6 OR B = 7) THEN GOSUB 70 : PRINT A$
   20 IF HIT THEN 700 − where HIT is a variable whose value is normally 0, but is set to −1 when a collision occurs.
   30 IF NOT(A=7 AND B=4) THEN 70

INPUT

    : statement

    : INPUT [variable list]

      INPUT [string];[variable list]

      [string] must be a string constant, e.g. "PROMPT"

      [variable list] may be 1 or more variables separated by commas

    : where there is no string, the user is prompted for input by a "?".
Where there is a string, this is printed, followed by ? . INPUT
differs from GET in that it waits for input, may accept more than
single characters, echoes input on the screen, and requires a
RETURN keypress to terminate input. Where the variable list
contains more than one variable, values must be typed separated
by commas. The values are assigned to the variables in order. If
the user types in too few values, the ? reappears and INPUT
waits for more input. If too many values are typed, the message
EXTRA IGNORED is displayed. This is not an error and
execution continues.

If [string] is too long (the prompt string has a maximum length of 20
characters), INPUT will read all of the string with the input when
the input is a string, or return a REDO FROM START otherwise,
so keep prompts reasonably short. If the user types in a value of
the wrong type for the variable it is to be assigned to, a REDO
FROM START message appears, and the user is prompted for
correct input by "?".

e.g. 10 INPUT A – displays "?" and waits for a number to be
    typed,   followed by RETURN key.

    20 INPUT B, C$ – displays "?", waits for a number followed
by a   comma, a string and RETURN key.

    30 INPUT "PRICE?"; D – displays "PRICE?", waits for
number,   RETURN key.

    Note: Cannot be used in immediate mode.

INPUT#

    : statement

    : INPUT# [file–number], [variable list]

    : accepts input from an OPENed file by reading that file into the
buffer and assigns each data item to a variable in the variable list,
in order. Data items must agree in number and type with the
variables in the variable list. If an end–of–record is read before all
variables in the variable list have been assigned values, an OUT
OF DATA status is generated but the program continues to
execute.

    INPUT# does not display error messages, it reports error
statuses, in the status byte, that the program must respond to.

    : because the input buffer is only 80 characters long, an input string, together with separator, cannot be longer than this. Commas and RETURNs act as separators. They cannot act as data – you need a GET# for that.

e.g. 10 OPEN 1,1 – default values used so this OPENs the datatsette

20 INPUT# 1,A$,C,D,E$ – and reads these from buffer.

Note: INPUT# can only be used in program mode.

INT

: function

: INT ([numeric variable, constant or expression])

: returns the largest integer less than or equal to the argument.

e.g. 10 PRINT INT(6.23) – displays 6

20 PRINT INT(–4.2)– displays –5

30 X% = INT(43.4) – assigns value 43 to X%

40 PRINT INT(14) – displays 14

50 PRINT INT(A) – displays integer value of A

LEFT$

: function

LEFT$ ([string variable, constant or expression] , [integer])

: returns a string consisting of the first [integer] characters of the original string argument. If [integer] is greater than the length of the string, the entire string is returned. If [integer] is 0, the null string is returned.

e.g. 10 A$ = "TEST STRING"

20 B$ = LEFT$(A$,4)

30 PRINT B$ – displays "TEST"

40 PRINT LEFT$("GOODBYE",3) – displays "GOO"

50 A$ = LEFT$(A$,3) + LEFT$(A$,4)

60 PRINT A$ – displays "TESTEST"

: LEFT$ is often used to postion the cursor. A string of cursor control characters is created which, when printed, moves the cursor across or down the screen. LEFT$ can then be used to control how far across or down the screen the cursor is positioned.

e.g. 10 A$ = "CRSR   CRSR   ..."

20 PRINT LEFT$(A$,10) – moves the cursor across the screen 10 spaces.

LEN

: function

: LEN ([string variable, constant or expression])

: returns the length of the string argument. Blanks and non–printing characters are counted.

e.g. PRINT LEN ("HARRY") - displays 5

10 A$ = "MIGHTY"

```
20 B$ = LEFT$ (A$,LEN$(A$)-1)
30 PRINT B$ - displays "MIGHT"
```

LET

: statement
: LET[variable] = [value]
: assigns the value on the right to the variable on the left. The word
  LET can be omitted, and so is rarely used.
  e.g. 10 LET A$ = "HELLO"
        20 A$ = HELLO - equivalent to line 10
        30 C$ = LEFT(A$,4) - assigns HELL to C$
        40 D$ = C$ - assigns value of C$ to D$

LIST

: statement
: LIST - displays entire program
: LIST [line-number] - displays line [line-number]
: LIST - [line-number] - displays from start of program to line
  [line-number] (inclusive)
: LIST [line-number] - - displays from line [line-number] to end
  of program
: LIST [line-number1] - [line-number2] - displays from line
  [line-number1] to [line-number2] (inclusive)
: displays all or part of the program in memory as detailed above. If
  the program exceeds the length of the screen display, the screen
  will scroll up. This may be slowed down by holding down the CTRL
  key, or stopped using the STOP key.
  e.g. LIST - 100
        LIST 50 - 999
        LIST 20
: If used in program mode, the program will stop after LISTing.
  Typing CONT at this point will only repeat the LISTing.

LOAD

: statement
: LOAD
  LOAD ["filename"]
  LOAD ["filename"],[device]
: transfers a program from cassette or disk into memory.
  If there are no arguments to LOAD, the next program found on
  tape will be LOADed.
  If there is a ["filename"], the Commodore 64 will search the tape
  until a program of that name is found, and load it. [device]
  specifies the device the program is loaded from. If it is 8, the
  program will be loaded from disk, if it is 1, from tape and if it is not
  present, the default value is 1, i.e. tape.

27

e.g. LOAD – loads next program on tape
LOAD "MYPROG" – searches tape for program called "MYPROG" and loads it if it is found.
LOAD A$ – searches tape for program whose name is the value of A$ and loads it.
LOAD "*" , 8 – loads first program found on disk.
LOAD "PR*" , 8 – loads first program whose name begins with "PR" from disk.
LOAD "NB" , 8 – finds program "NB" on disk and loads it.
: When used in immediate mode, a CLR statement is automatically executed. When used in program mode, if the new program is shorter than the old one, variables will not be cleared, so the new program may use the old variable values.

LOG

: function
: LOG ([numeric variable, constant or expression])
: the argument to LOG must be greater than 0
: returns the natural logarithm of the argument, ie. the power to which **e** must be raised to give the argument.
e.g. 10 PRINT LOG(6.42856) – displays 1.86075056

MID$

: function
: MID$ ([string variable, constant or expression],[from],[length])
  MID$ ([string variable, constant or expression],[from])
: returns a string of length [length] consisting of the characters starting from the [from]th character of the string argument. If [length] is omitted, returns the entire string from the [from]th character on. If [length] is greater than the length of the string argument, the null string is returned.
e.g. 10 PRINT MID$("HELLO",2,3) – displays "ELL"
20 PRINT MID$("GOODBYE",1,4,) – displays "GOOD"
30 X$ = "HATTRICK"
40 PRINT MID$(X$,4) – displays "TRICK"

NEW

: statement
: clears program from memory and resets variables
e.g. X = 6.2
PRINT X – displays 6.2
NEW
PRINT X – displays 0. Old value of X is lost as are any program lines.
: Using NEW in program mode will clear the program in which it is a program statement.

NOT

  : logical operator
  : NOT [expression or variable]
  : logically negates the truth value of [expression]
  : 10 IF NOT(A=6 AND B=9) THEN 70
  If the expression (A=6 AND B=9) is false then NOT(A=6 AND B=9) is true and the program branches to 70.
  20 IF NOT HIT THEN GOSUB 500
  Assume HIT is a variable set to −1 when a collision between game characters occurs, 0 otherwise. Then NOT HIT will evaluate to true when there is no collision, and the appropriate action (subroutine 500) can be taken.
  NOTE: NOT can also operate on other numeric values (see p 15).

ON

  : statement
  : ON [variable or expression] GOTO [line−number list]
  ON [variable or expression] GOSUB [line−number list]
  [line−number list] is a series of line−numbers separated by commas
  : causes the program to branch to one of the line−numbers depending on the value of the ON argument. If the argument evaluates to 1, the program branches to the first line−number, if 2 then it branches to the second line−number, etc. If the argument evaluates to 0 or to a number greater than the number of line−numbers then the statement is ignored. If the argument evaluates to a negative number an error occurs.
  e.g. 10 ON X%+3 GOTO 50,72,143,90
     20 ON B% GOSUB 70,90,90,300
     30 ON INT(B*C/3) GOTO 20,60,90,15

OPEN

  :statement
  :OPEN [file−number]
  OPEN [file−number],[device−number]
  OPEN [file−number],[device−number],[command−number]
  OPEN [file−number] , [device−number] , [command−number] , [string]
  :OPENs a logical channel for input or output to a device. When a channel is OPENed to an external device, a buffer is automatically set up. Transmission and receipt of data occurs a whole buffer at a time.
  [file−number] is the logical name of the channel, It can be any number in the range 1−255, and is the same number used in INPUT#, GET#, PRINT# and CLOSE statements to work with this device.

[device – number] specifies the device as below:

Device Number	Device
0	keyboard
1	cassette - default device
2	RS232 device
3	screen
4	printer
5	printer
8	disk drive
4-127	serial bus device
128-255	serial bus device - and send a linefeed (lf) after carriage return.

: [command – number] must be in the range 0–255. The same command number will have different effects depending on the device specified.

Device	Command Number	Effect
Cassette	0	read tape file
	1	write tape file
	2	write tape file and put EOT (end of tape) marker when channel CLOSEd
Disk	1 - 14	open data channel
	15	open command channel
Keyboard	1 - 255	no effect
Screen	1 - 255	no effect
Printer	0	upper case/graphics
	7	upper/lower case

: [string] is sent to the printer or screen as if a PRINT# were performed to the device. With the cassette deck it is used as the filename. With the disk drive it can be either a filename or a command, depending on the command number.

e.g. OPEN 1,0 – open channel to keyboard

OPEN 1,1,0 – open channel to cassette for reading only

OPEN 1,1,0, MYPROG – open channel to cassette for reading only. When a read is done, the Commodore 64 will search tape for "MYPROG"

OPEN 1,3 – open read/write channel to screen

OPEN 1,8,15, command – open channel to disk and send command

OR

: logical operator

: [expression] OR [expression]

: produces a true result (−1) if either or both of the expression are true, a false result (0) only if both expression are false

e.g. 10 IF (A=6 OR B$="NO") THEN 90
20 IF (HIT% OR B=6) THEN GOSUB 60
NOTE: OR can also operate on numeric values (see p 15).

PEEK

: function

: PEEK ([address])

: returns the contents, in decimal, of the byte named by [address]. In those sections of memory where there is a ROM/RAM overlay only the ROM at that address will be PEEKed. To PEEK the RAM, the ROM must be switched out.

e.g. 10 PRINT PEEK(53280) – displays the value of the screen border colour byte.
20 PRINT PEEK(651) – displays the value of a counter controlling the time a key must be pressed before it repeats automatically

POKE

: statement

: POKE [address],[value]

: puts [value] into the byte at [address]. [value] must be in the range 0 to 255. Unlike PEEK, which will return the contents of any address in memory, either ROM or RAM, POKE will only change the contents of RAM. If a value is POKEd into an area of memory where there is a ROM/RAM overlay, the RAM is automatically accessed, whether or not the ROM is switched out.

e.g. POKE 65514,15 POKEs a value into the RAM under the KERNAL ROM.

POS

: function

: POS ([dummy])

the value of the dummy argument may be anything as it's not used.

: returns the cursor's position in a line. Since a logical line may be up to 80 characters long, a value betweeen 0 and 80 may be returned.

If no cursor is being displayed, e.g. during a string manipulation in a program, the position of the character currently being handled is returned. Since a string of up to 255 characters may be built using concatenation, a value in the range 0–255 will be returned.

e.g. PRINT "CURSOR AT";POS(0) – displays "CURSOR AT 9"

31

PRINT

    : statement

    : PRINT [argument]

      PRINT [argument], [argument] ...

      PRINT [argument]; [argument] ...

    : displays the arguments listed after PRINT. If the arguments are separated by a comma, the Commodore 64 reserves 11 spaces for the arguments, so displays may be widely separated. If the arguments are separated by semi-colons, there is no separation between arguments.

After each PRINT statement the cursor automatically moves to the next line. This can be stopped by finishing the PRINT statement with a comma or semi–colon.

String arguments to PRINT may contain special characters such as cursor control and colours. These characters appear in the string as reversed characters. (See Appendix C) Where the PRINT statement is executed, the special characters carry out their function. They are not displayed.

"Programmable" cursor controls are CRSR ↑, CRSR ↓, CRSR ←, CRSR →, CLR, HOME, INST. Some special characters need different treatment, however. For example, DEL and RETURN operate normally when an attempt is made to put either in a string, and quote marks will terminate the string.

As you have probably found out, pressing DEL deletes a character but you might at some time want to program it into a string. The following steps show how to achieve this:

1)   Terminate the string with quotation marks. e.g. "STRING"

2)   Press DEL – this will delete the closing quotation marks but leave you out of quote mode.

3)   Press INST as many times as you want to insert a DEL, say twice.

4)   Now press DEL twice. These DELs will display as reversed characters and will not execute yet.

5)   Now put in replacement letters, if any, and complete the string with quote marks.

All your keypresses should look something like this:

"STRING" start with completed string

press DEL to remove quotemark

press INST twice to insert 2 DELs

press DEL twice

Add replacement letters, in this case FE

close quotation marks

The display should now look like this:

e.g. 10 PRINT "STRING 🚇 🚇 FE"

      and when executed will display "STRIFE"

When LISTed the string looks as it displays, so editing can be difficult if you've forgotten what you've done.

Other special characters can be put into strings in the following way:

(i)   Type the string, and RETURN key, leaving spaces for characters to be added later

(ii)   Use cursor control keys to get back to the space

(iii)   Press CTRL, RVSON

(iv)   Press the keys corresponding to the special character you want, as shown below:

Character	Type
Shift Return	SHIFT M
switch to lower case	N
switch to upper case	SHIFT N
disable case switching keys	H
enable case switching keys	I

: The Shift Return character, like DEL executes when LISTed, so editing will again be difficult.

A more general, easier to remember, and more obvious method of "programming" special characters is to use CHR$ and concatenation.

Note: PRINT can be abreviated to "?"

e.g. PRINT 50

    10 PRINT A$, 60; B

    20 ? "A STRING" ; 24 ; "LETTERS LONG"

    30 PRINT "LATEST PROGRAM"

    40 FOR J=0 TO 1000 : NEXT

    50 ? "CRSR ↓ CRSR → CRSR → CRSR ← CRSR →

    "DEL INST INST DEL DEL"

Lines 30—50 will display "LATEST PROGRAM", wait, and change it to "LAST PROGRAM". Line 50 will not look like this when you type it in. As written , it indicates the keys you press.

PRINT#

: statement

: PRINT# [file−number],[variable list]

: similar to PRINT, but sends the contents of the variable list to a device which has been previously OPENed. The variable list is transmitted in the same format as it would be PRINTed to the screen. If commas are used to separate variables, extra spaces are sent, if semi−colons are used, no spaces are transmitted. The commas and semi−colons are not themselves PRINT#ed.

If no comma or semi−colon appears at the end of the variable list a CHR$(13) (RETURN) is sent. It is probably best to separate

33

variables with CHR$(13) on the file so that INPUT$ can be used to read them back.

e.g. 10 OPEN 1,1,1,"Data File"
20 RT$ = CHR$(13)
30 PRINT#1, LOW SCORE ;RT$;LS;RT$; HIGH SCORE
40 PRINT#1, AVERAGE ;RT$;A$
50 CLOSE 1

OPENing the file clears the tape buffer ready for data. The buffer retains the data until it is cleared by a statement that does this as a part of its execution, like OPEN. Commas and semi−colons may also be used to separate variables on the file. these must be explicitly PRINT#ed as the RETURNS were in the example above.

READ

: statement
: READ [variable list]
variables in the list are separated by commas
: reads data from DATA statements and assigns each data item to the next variable in the variable list. When there is no unread data in DATA statements and a READ is attempted, an "OUT OF DATA" error occurs and the program aborts.

DATA statements are read in order of ascending line number. Within a DATA statement, data is read sequentially from left to right. The Commodore 64 increments a DATA pointer after each element is read. If a RESTORE statement is used, the DATA pointer is reset to point to the first data item of the first DATA statement.

e.g. 20 READ A, C$, B, D$
60 DATA 6.4, HISCORE, 2.6, LOSCORE
When new data items are assigned to a variable, the old value is lost.
70 READ C$, C$
80 DATA HI, BYE
Final value of C$ is "BYE"
90 FOR J=0 TO 5
100 READ A(J) : NEXT
110 DATA 1, 2, 3, 6, 9

REM

: statement
: REM[text]
: no effect − REM statements are ignored by BASIC. They are provided to enable programmers to include comments about the program.

If graphics characters are used in a REM statement they must be preceded by quote marks, otherwise they will be interpreted as BASIC keywords.

REM statements may appear as the last statement on a multiple statement line. If they are not last, any statements following them on the line will be ignored.

e.g. 20 REM 20–160 CALCULATE GROSS WAGES
      150 GOTO 200 :REM BRANCH TO "HIT" SUBROUTINE

RESTORE

: statement
: RESTORE
: each time a READ is executed, the DATA pointer is advanced to point to the next DATA item. RESTORE resets the DATA pointer to the first data item of the first DATA statement.

e.g. 10 FOR J=1 TO 5
      20 READ(A$) : NEXT
      30 RESTORE
      40 FOR J= 6 TO 12
      50 READ A$(J) : NEXT
      60 DATA A,B,C,D,E,F,G

RIGHT$

: function
: RIGHT$ ([string variable, constant or expression],[number])
: returns the string consisting of the rightmost [number] of characters of the original string. If [number] equals the length of the string, the entire string is returned. If [number] equals 0, the null string is returned.

e.g. 10 ? RIGHT$("FRANTIC" , 5) – displays "ANTIC"
      20 ? RIGHT$(A$, LEN(A$)–1) – displays all but the leftmost character of A$

RND

: function
: RND ([number])
: returns a pseudo–random number between 0 and 1 (not including 1), by performing calculations on a 'seed' value. If the argument is positive the same pseudo-random sequence is generated for a given seed. If the argument is negative, the function is re-seeded with each function call. If the argument is 0, a number is generated from the system clock.

A seed is generated on power-up and stored in locations 139-143.

e.g. 10 REM SUBROUTINE FOR RANDOM DICE THROW
20 T1 = RND(0) — get random number between 0 and 1
30 T2 = (T1*6)+1 — change to range 1 — 6.9999...
40 THROW = INT(T2) — get integer value of throw
This could, of course, be done on one line.
20 THROW = INT(RND(0)*6)+1

SAVE

: statement
: SAVE
SAVE ["filename"]
SAVE ["filename"],[device]
SAVE ["filename"],[device],[command]

: saves the program currently in memory onto cassette tape or diskette.

If there are no arguments to SAVE, the program is saved to tape with no name. If the [filename] is given, the program is saved to tape under that name.

[device] specifies tape (using code 1) or diskette (using code 8).
[command] may be:

1) — when loaded the program will go into the same part of memory it came from.

2) — an end—of—tape marker will be written after the program. When the Commodore 64 reads this at a later date, it will act as though it has reached the end of the tape. If, for example, it is searching for a file which was written onto tape after the end-of-tape marker, it will stop and display a "DEVICE NOT PRESENT" message when it reads the EOT marker.

3) — combination of 1 and 2.

e.g. SAVE
SAVE "GAME1" — saves GAME1 on tape
SAVE G$ — saves on tape with the value of G$ as name
SAVE "GAME2",8 — saves "GAME2" on diskette
SAVE "GAME3",1,1 — saves on tape — will reload into same part of memory.
SAVE "GAME4",1,3 — saves on tape — adds EOT marker — will reload into same part of memory.

Usually used in immediate mode, but can be used in program mode. The program will continue normally after SAVEing.

SGN

: function
: SGN ([number])
: if [number] less than 0 returns —1
if [number] equal to 0 returns 0

if [number] greater than 0 returns 1
e.g. 20 IF SGN(X) = 1 THEN 60
        30 ON SGN(X)+2 GOSUB 100, 200, 300

SIN

: function
: SIN ([number])
: returns the sine of the argument, which is in radians
e.g. 20 ? SIN(1.5) − displays .997494987

SPC

: function
: SPC ([number])
: prints [number] spaces on the screen. [number] must be between 0 and 255. SPC can only used with PRINT.
: 20 PRINT "LEFT" ; SPC (7) : "RIGHT"
PRINT SPC (21) ; "!"

SQR

: function
: SQR ([number])
: returns the square root of [number] , [number] must be greater than or equal to 0
e.g. 10 PRINT SQR (4) - displays 2
        20 A = 64
        30 ? SQR (A) - displays 8
        40 ? SQR (A * A) - displays 64

STATUS

: function
: STATUS or
ST
: returns a value corresponding to the state of the last input/output operation. Different bits of the status byte are set on different conditions, as shown below:

BIT	VALUE	CASSETTE READ	SERIAL BUS R/W	TAPE VERIFY AND LOAD
0	1		time out write	
1	2		time out read	
2	4	short block		short block
3	8	long block		long block
4	16	unrecoverable read error		any mismatch
5	32	check sum error		check sum error
6	64	end of file	E01	
7	−128	end of tape	device not present	end of tape

37

```
e.g.  10 OPEN 1, 1, 0, "DATA"
      20 GET# 1, A$
      30 IF STATUS = 64 THEN 60
      40 PRINT A$
      50 GOTO 20
      60 PRINT A$ : CLOSE 1
```

NOTE: The status byte is located at 144.

STOP

: statement
: STOP
: halts a program and returns control to the user. The only
  difference between STOP and END statements is that the STOP
  statement produces the message "BREAK IN [line-number]".
  Thus, with more than one STOP in a program, you can be sure
  which one has been reached. As with the END statement,
  variables can be examined and changed and the program
  continued with CONT.
  e.g. 70 STOP - displays "BREAK IN 70" and halts.

STR$

: function
: STR$ ([numeric constant, variable or expression])
: returns the string representation of the value of the argument.
  e.g. 10 ? STR$ (57.42) - displays "57.42"
        20 ? STR$ (−73) - displays "−73"
        30 ? STR$ (2E + 2) - displays "200"
        40 ? STR$ (3E + 10) - displays "3E + 10"
        50 A = 67.24
        60 ? STR$ (A) - displays " 67.24"
: Note that positive numbers have a leading space reserved for the
  sign so when STR$ed they are longer than they look.
  e.g. 70 ? LEN (STR$ (72)) - displays 3

SYS

: statement
: SYS [address]
: in effect, performs a GOSUB to the machine language program
  starting at [address]. This is the most common way to mix BASIC
  and machine language programs.
  The VIC20 already has useful machine language routines (Kernal
  routines) which can be accessed via SYS. Also, users may POKE
  their own machine language routines into memory and access
  them with SYS.
  e.g. 20 SYS 65508 - gets character from keyboard buffer
        30 SYS 40800 - jumps to routine previously POKEd into
        memory at address 40800, and returns.
    NOTE: See machine language programming chapter 6.

TAB

: function
: TAB ([numeric variable, constant or expression])
: moves cursor to the position in a logical line given by the argument. If the cursor is already past that position on the current line, it is moved to that position on the next line. The leftmost position on the screen is 0. The TAB argument must be in the range 0 — 255. TAB must be used with a PRINT statement.
  e.g.   20 PRINT "NAME" ; TAB (8) ; "ADDRESS"

TAN

: function
: TAN ([numeric variable, constant or expression])
: returns the tangent of the argument, which is in radians.
  e.g.   20 PRINT TAN (1.642)

TIME

: function
: TIME or
  TI
: returns the value of an internal clock which counts intervals of one sixtieth of a second (jiffies). This is initialized on start-up and reset to 0 after 51,839,999 increments. This may be useful for timing program segments. Note that it is turned off during tape I/O.
  e.g.   20 X = TI : GOSUB 600
          30 ET = (TI — X) / 60
          40 ? "subroutine 600 took";
          50 ? ET ; "seconds to execute"

TIME$

: function
: TIME$ or
  TI$
: returns a 6 character string indicating hours, minutes, seconds — i.e. "HH MM SS" — on a 24 hour clock. The correct time must be initialized by the user. It is lost when the Commodore 64 is turned off, and will not be accurate after tape I/O.
  e.g.   20 TI$ = "131500" — initialize to 1.15 pm.
          30 IF TI$ < > "131559" THEN 30
          40 ? "WAKE UP"

USR

: function
: USR ([arg])
: calls a user written machine language subroutine, whose starting address is stored at memory addresses 785 and 786 (low byte in 785, high byte in 786). To calculate the POKE values for each

39

address byte, find the address in Hex and convert each byte to decimal. The [arg] is initially stored in the floating point accumulator (memory locations 97 — 102), and the result returned is the final value stored in the accumulator.

e.g. 20 POKE 785, 0 : POKE 786; 144 — poke start address (9000 Hex = 36864 decimal)

30 A = USR (3) — call subroutine, assign result to A

VAL

: function

: VAL ([string constant, variable or expression])

: returns the numerical value of the string argument. If the string does not start with +, −, . or a digit, the function returns 0

e.g. 20 INPUT "PRICE" ; A$

30 PR = VAL (A$)

40 IF PR = 0 THEN PRINT "NUMBER EXPECTED" : GOTO 20

50 ? VAL ("73.2") — displays 73.2

60 ? VAL ("7" + "3" + "." + "2") — displays 73.2

70 ? VAL (STR$ (73.2)) — displays 0, since STR$ returns "[space] 73.2"

80 ? VAL (MID$ (STR$ (73.2) , 2)) — displays 73.2

VERIFY

: statement

: VERIFY

VERIFY ["filename"]

VERIFY ["filename"] , [device]

: checks the program on tape or diskette against the program currently in memory, and displays the message "VERIFY ERROR" if they don't match. This is used to ensure that a program has been SAVEd properly. Make a habit of VERIFYing immediately after SAVEing.

When there are no arguments in VERIFY, it checks the next program it finds on tape. When ["filename"] appears as argument, the program of that name is searched for on tape and VERIFYd, if found.

[device] is used to VERIFY a program saved on diskette. As usual [device] is 8 for the disk drive, 1 for cassette (default).

e.g. VERIFY — checks next program on tape

VERIFY "MYPROG" — searches for "MYPROG" on tape and VERIFYs it, if found.

VERIFY "HERPROG", 8 — searches for "HERPROG" on diskette, and VERIFYs it, if found.

: Don't forget to rewind the tape after SAVEing so that the relevant program can be found.

WAIT

: statement

: WAIT [address] , [mask1]

  WAIT [address] , [mask1] , [mask2]

: causes the program to wait until the value in [address] changes in a way specified by [mask1] and [mask2].

The value in [address] is bitwise ANDed with the value in [mask1]. If there is a [mask2], the result of the AND is exclusively ORed with the value in [mask2].

Exclusive OR is different to the OR met previously, which is included. Exclusive OR (XOR) only produces a true result when only 1 of its arguments is true, a false result otherwise.

i.e. 1 XOR 1 = 0 — false

      1 XOR 0 = 1 — true

      0 XOR 1 = 1 — true

      0 XOR 0 = 0 — false

: If the result of the AND and XOR is 0, WAIT continues to wait. If the result is not 0, execution proceeds normally from the statement following the WAIT. This statement is generally used to monitor I/O activities. A novice programmer is unlikely to need it.

e.g. 20 WAIT 160, 144, 128 (160 is 1 byte of the 3-byte jiffie clock which is continually changing its values.)

: This will cause the program to wait until bit 8 of 160 is off (0) or bit 5 is on (1) or both.

(See page 16 for more on bit, bytes and masks.)

CHAPTER 3

Compressing BASIC Programs

It may sometimes be desirable to compress programs. The following is a list of methods you can use to do this

Abbreviating Keywords

Most BASIC keywords can be abbreviated as shown in the table on pages 43, 44. Using these does not directly save memory, since keywords are stored as tokens, not the actual word. However, it means that it is possible to put more information on a line, thus reducing the number of line-numbers, which do use extra memory. It also cuts typing time. Abbreviations are expanded to the full word when LISTed.

Multiple statement lines.

These help minimize the number of line-numbers needed. The only limitation is that a multiple statement line should not exceed 80 characters, including colons and RETURN.

Variables.

Keep variable names short.

When a number, word or string is used often in a program, it should be assigned as the value of a variable, which can then be used in its place.

```
e.g.  10 A = 36874
      20 POKE A,13 : POKE A,72 : POKE A,16
```
This has the added advantage of enabling you to squeeze more on a line, and, again, cuts typing time.

READ, DATA statement

When a repetitive task, such as defining your own character set, needs to be done, it is more memory efficient to use DATA statements to hold the values together with a READ statement in a loop, than to write all the individual repetitions.

```
e.g.  10 FOR J = 0 TO 63
      20 READ A,V : POKE A,V : NEXT
      30 DATA 12288, 0, 12289, 48, 12290, 128 ...
      40 DATA ...
```
rather than
```
      10 POKE 12288,0 : POKE 12289,48 : POKE 12290,128

      ...
      70 ... POKE 12351,0
```

Arrays

These can be used for the same purpose as DATA statements. Where possible, use integer arrays rather than floating point arrays, since elements use 2 bytes compared with 5 for floating point elements.

Spaces

The BASIC interpreter does not need spaces in programs, but if used they are stored. Eliminating them therefore saves memory. It also makes programs difficult to read, so this is best done after all debugging.

GOSUB

Using subroutines obviously saves memory, since it saves writing the same section of code several times. You should note however, that GOSUBs can be fairly slow, since it must stack and retrieve addresses.

TAB, SPC

These two functions may be more economical than a string of cursor control commands to position a character on the screen.

REM statements

These may be removed entirely once the program is debugged and read for use. This isn't a great idea, since you may have to examine or change the program at a later date, but it does save space.

Overlays

This involves breaking programs up into sections which are loaded in sequence. For example, many games programs involve defining a new character set. Instead of having 1 program which both defines the character set and runs the game, 2 programs can be written. The first defines the character set and then LOADs the second program, which runs the game, on top of it. Many programs have such initialization tasks to do, and overlays can be useful in these cases - arrays and variables can be defined and given values by one program and used by another. However, a limitation is that the second program must be shorter than the first program otherwise it will overwrite the variable values.

Abbreviations for BASIC keywords

Command	Abbreviation	Command	Abbreviation
ABS	A SHIFT B	OPEN	O SHIFT P
AND	A SHIFT N	PEEK	P SHIFT E
ASC	A SHIFT S	POKE	P SHIFT O
ATN	A SHIFT T	PRINT	?
CHR$	C SHIFT C	PRINT#	P SHIFT R
CLOSE	CL SHIFT O	READ	R SHIFT E
CLR	C SHIFT L	RESTORE	RE SHIFT S
CMD	C SHIFT M	RETURN	RE SHIFT T
CONT	C SHIFT O	RIGHT$	R SHIFT I

Keyword	Abbreviation	Keyword	Abbreviation
DATA	D SHIFT A	RND	R SHIFT N
DEF	D SHIFT E	RUN	R SHIFT U
DIM	D SHIFT I	SAVE	S SHIFT A
END	E SHIFT N	SGN	S SHIFT G
EXP	E SHIFT X	SIN	S SHIFT I
FOR	F SHIFT O	SPC(*	S SHIFT P
FRE	F SHIFT R	SQR	S SHIFT Q
GET	G SHIFT E	STEP	ST SHIFT E
GOSUB	GO SHIFT S	STOP	S SHIFT T
GOTO	G SHIFT O	STR$	ST SHIFT R
INPUT#	I SHIFT N	SYS	S SHIFT Y
LET	L SHIFT E	TAB(*	T SHIFT A
LEFT$	LE SHIFT F	THEN	T SHIFT H
LIST	L SHIFT I	USR	U SHIFT S
LOAD	L SHIFT O	VAL	V SHIFT A
MID$	M SHIFT I	VERIFY	V SHIFT E
NEXT	N SHIFT E	WAIT	W SHIFT A
NOT	N SHIFT O		

* Take care not to put in another left parenthesis.

Appending BASIC programs

So far, whenever you have loaded a BASIC program it has overwritten the program in memory. However, because the Commodore 64 relies on pointers to tell it where the start of program memory is, it is possible to load in a program and join it to the program already in memory.

The start of program memory pointer resides at locations 43 and 44. Type PRINT PEEK(43), PEEK(44) in direct mode. The normal values are 1 and 8. To change the pointer to point to the end of the program currently in memory, type:

    POKE 43, PEEK(45) − 2 : POKE 44, PEEK(46)

Now the next program to be loaded will start at the end of the first program. To make the Commodore 64 see both programs as one, reset the pointer to the original value using

    POKE 43,1 : POKE 44,8

The only restriction to this technique is that the second program to be loaded must have higher line numbers than the program already in memory.

This technique will enable you to save common subroutines independently and add them to programs when needed.

BASIC program storage format

Program lines are sorted from the start of the BASIC user area in order of ascending line numbers. Variable storage starts from the end of the program . Array storage starts from the end of variable storage. String storage starts at the top end of available user memory and works down towards the end of array storage.

The following pointers are used to keep track of storage.

Pointer Address	Use	Default
43,44	Start of BASIC area	2048
45,46	Start of BASIC variables	—
47,48	Start of arrays	—
49,50	End of arrays	—
53,54	End of strings	—
51,52	Start of strings	40960
55,56	Highest address used by BASIC	40960
65,66	Current DATA item	—

Program lines are compressed before being stored. That is, keywords are tokenized - converted into a one byte code. Each line is then stored in the following format.

Link Address	Line-nr.	BASIC TEXT	End-of-line
Lo-byte Hi-byte	Lo-byte Hi-byte		0

The link address points to the start of the next line. The line number is a 2-byte binary number from 1 to 63999. Line numbers in the BASIC text (as arguments of GOTO, GOSUB) are stored in ASCII format - 1 byte per digit. The end of the line is indicated by a 0 byte. The end of the program is indicated by a 00 link address.

Worry-free overlays and the keyboard buffer

When overlays were previously mentioned, one of the restrictions was that the overlay had to be shorter than the program it was loaded over. Using the keyboard buffer bypasses this restriction, and makes the use of overlays tidier. The program lines below should be added to the end of a program to be overlaid.

```
60000  POKE 631 , 78 : POKE 632 , 69 : POKE 633 , 87 : POKE 634
       , 13 : POKE 635 , 76 : POKE 636 , 111 : POKE 637 , 13
60001  POKE 638 , 82 : POKE 639 , 117 : POKE 640 , 13 : POKE
       198 , 10
```

These lines POKE into the buffer the abbreviations for the commands NEW, LOAD and RUN, each followed by a RETURN. Thus the old

45

program is cleared out, the overlay loaded in and run, all without the user having to do anything and without the programmer having to worry about the size of the overlay.

Commodore 64 BASIC Keyword Codes

Character/ Keyword	Code (decimal)	Character/ Keyword	Code (decimal)	Character/ Keyword	Code (decimal)
end-of-line	0	POKE	151	=	178
unused	1-31	PRINT#	152		179
same as		PRINT	153	SGN	180
CHR$	32-95	CONT	154	INT	181
codes		LIST	155	ABS	182
unused	96-127	CLR	156	USR	183
END	128	CMD	157	FRE	184
FOR	129	SYS	158	POS	185
NEXT	130	OPEN	159	SQR	186
DATA	131	CLOSE	160	RND	187
INPUT#	132	GET	161	LOG	188
INPUT	133	NEW	162	EXP	189
DIM	134	TAB(	163	COS	190
READ	135	TO	164	SIN	191
LET	136	FN	165	TAN	192
GOTO	137	SPC(	166	ATN	193
RUN	138	THEN	167	PEEK	194
IF	139	NOT	168	LEN	195
RESTORE	140	STEP	169	STR$	196
GOSUB	141	+	170	VAL	197
RETURN	142	–	171	ASC	198
REM	143	*	172	CHR$	199
STOP	144	/	175	LEFT$	200
ON	145	↑	174	RIGHT$	201
WAIT	146	AND	175	MID$	202
LOAD	147	OR	176	unused	203-254
SAVE	148		177		255
VERIFY	149				
DEF	150				

Codes are interpreted according to this table except when characters are in a string, when CHR$ codes apply. Arithmetic and relational operators are interpreted as keywords unless they appear in a string.

Clearing the keyboard buffer.

If you are using PEEK (197) to find the current keystroke, the keyboard buffer will fill up. Thus, the next time the Commodore 64 looks at the keyboard buffer it will find either meaningless or misleading data. This can, under certain circumstances, cause problems. You should therefore be aware that you can clear the keyboard buffer when necessary.

The buffer is located at addresses 631-340.

The number of characters currently in the buffer is held at address 198.

The simplest way to clear the buffer is to POKE 0 into 198.

i.e.   POKE 198,0

The keyboard buffer can also be used in a more positive fashion. Program lines can be added and changed from within a program. For example, the following program allows the user to input functions, have them defined using DEF FN and then have them evaluated.

This program is a self-modifying program, creating a new line 100 each time a new function (X$) is entered.

```
5 REM *** DEFINING FUNCTIONS ***
10 PRINT"ENTER FUNCTION OF X"
20 INPUT X$
30 POKE198,3:POKE631,19:POKE632,13:POKE633,13
40 PRINT"[CLR]100DEFFNA(X)="X$":RETURN"
50 PRINT"[HOME]GOTO 60":SYS 42115:REM 42115 IS BASIC
   WARM START ROUTINE
60 GOSUB 100
70 INPUT "[DOWN]ENTER X";X:PRINT"FN(X)="FNA(X):
   GOTO 70
```

Explanation

Line 30 : sets the number of characters in the buffer and puts two returns in there.

Line 40 : prints line 100, substituting the input function for X$.

Line 50 : prints GOTO 60, homes the cursor and ends the program.

With the program over, the characters in the keyboard buffer are executed. The first return enters line 100 into the program. The second causes the immediate command GOTO 60 to be executed, thus re-entering the program.

Line 60 : causes the function to be defined.

Line 70 : evaluates the function at points input by the user.

Window Listing

The same technique can be used to create a program which will list programs one line at a time and allow the user to move forwards and backwards through the listing. Mistakes must be noted and corrected **after** exiting from this program.

To use it, append it to the program to be listed, as described in the section on appending BASIC programs, and type RUN 60000

```
60000 SA=PEEK(44)*256+PEEK(43)-1:FL=SA
60002 LN=PEEK(SA+3)+PEEK(SA+4)*256
60003 PRINT"◼GOTO60010":PRINT"LIST";LN
60004 POKE631,19:POKE632,17:POKE633,154:POKE634,
13:POKE635,19:POKE636,13:POKE198,6:END
60010 IF PEEK(197)=40 THEN 60100:REM TEST "+"
KEY
60020 IF PEEK(197)=43 THEN 60200:REM TEST "-"
KEY
60030 GOTO 60010
60100 REM "+"ACTION
60105 TE=(PEEK(SA+1)+PEEK(SA+2)*256)-1
60110 IF (PEEK(TE+1)+PEEK(TE+2)*256)<>0 THEN
SA=TE
60120 GOTO 60002
60200 REM "-" KEY ACTION
60210 IF SA=FL THEN 60002
60220 SA=SA-1:IF PEEK(SA)=0 AND (SA-4)<>0 AND
PEEK(SA-3)<>0 THEN 60002
60230 GOTO 60210
```

Before reSAVEing the program reviewed, lines 60000-60230 should be deleted to avoid saving the program above as well.

Autonumber

The following program also uses the keyboard buffer in a similar manner. In this case to provide automatic numbering of BASIC program lines. Type RUN 60000 to run it.

```
60000 POKE56,159:POKE52,159:CLR
60010 INPUT"START";SA
60020 HS=INT(SA/256):LS=SA-HS*256
60030 INPUT"INCREMENT";IN:PRINT"◻"
60040 HI=INT(IN/256):LI=IN-HI*256
60050 POKE40705,LS:POKE40706,HS:POKE40707,LI:
POKE40708,HI
60060 SA=PEEK(40706)*256+PEEK(40705):IN=PEEK
(40708)*256+PEEK(40707)
60070 PRINT"◻"SA;"▮▮      ▮▮▮▮";:SA=SA+IN:POKE
40706,INT(SA/256)
60075 POKE40705,(SA-INT(SA/256)*256)
60077 POKE204,0
60080 GET K$:IF K$="" THEN 60080
60090 POKE207,0:PRINTK$;:POKE207,255:IF K$<>
CHR$(13) THEN 60080
```

48

```
60100 POKE631,145:POKE632,13:POKE633,71:POKE634,
111:POKE635,54:POKE636,48
60110 POKE637,48:POKE638,54:POKE639,48:POKE640,
13:POKE198,10:SYS42115
```

Before saving the program written, lines 60000-60100 should be deleted
to avoid saving the program above as well.

Machine Language merge program

Merge program for a Commodore 64. The machine code routine is totally
relocatable. If you wish to locate the routine at an address other than
40705, then lines 10 and 20 should be changed.

```
10 POKE 55,0:POKE56,159:CLR
20 S=40705:FOR J=S TO S+78:READ V
30 C=C+V:POKE J,V:NEXT
40 IFC<>8756THENPRINT"DATA ERROR":END
120 DATA 169,0,133,10,32,212,225,165
130 DATA 43,72,165,44,72,56,165,45
140 DATA 233,2,133,43,165,46,233,0
150 DATA 133,44,169,0,133,185,166,43
160 DATA 164,44,169,0,32,213,255,176
170 DATA 14,134,45,132,46,32,51,165
180 DATA 104,133,44,104,133,43,96,170
190 DATA 201,4,144,244,240,10,104,133
200 DATA 44,104,133,43,24,108,0,3
210 DATA 164,186,136,240,209,209,239
300 NEW
```

Using Merge

If the computer has just been turned on and you intend to merge two or
more programs, then use Method A. If you already have a program in
memory and you need to merge in another program, then use Method B.

When using the following method, remember to load in the program with
the lowest line numbers first.

Method A:
1. Type in Merge (or load merge if it has already been typed in and
saved)
2. Save Merge (if not already saved)
3. Run Merge

4. Load in first program
5. Type SYS 40705 "second program", device number
6. Repeat '5' for any other programs to be merged

Method B:
1. Save and verify the program currently residing in memory
2. Type NEW
3. Now use Method A

Block delete

When a large block of line numbers are to be deleted; using the method of entering the line number and hitting the RETURN key for each line can be time consuming and dangerous. The following routine once MERGEd can be executed by typing RUN 60000. The prompt "FROM, TO, STEP" will be displayed. Answer the prompt with the first and last line of the block to be deleted and the step-size between each line. (Use step-size 1 to delete all lines of block.)

```
60000 REM * BLOCK DELETE * (ROUTINE)
60010 INPUT"FROM,TO,STEP";F,T,S:PRINTCHR$(147)
60020 PRINTCHR$(19)F:F=F+S:PRINT"60040 F="F":
T="T":S="S:PRINT"GOTO60040"
60030 POKE 631,19:POKE632,13:POKE633,13:POKE
634,13:POKE 198,4:END
60040 F= 40 :T= 30 :S= 10
60050 IF F>T THEN PRINTCHR$(147):END
60060 GOTO 60020
```

CHAPTER 4

SOUND

THE 6581 SOUND INTERFACE DEVICE (SID)

The Commodore 64 uses a very powerful sound chip called the 6581. The sound chip has many powerful features each of which will be discussed in detail throughout this chapter. Each of the sound chip's registers (special memory locations within the chip) have been memory mapped to the Commodore's memory. A detailed memory map of these locations can be found at the end of this chapter.

WAVEFORMS

The tonal quality of a sound is determined by its waveform. Sound is made up of vibrations and the shape of each vibration determines the sound's waveform (the frequency of vibration determines the pitch.) The perfect vibration is a sine wave. The smooth rise and fall of a sine wave characterizes the smoothness of the sound produced by a sine wave. The same applies to other waveforms. The following waveforms are those used on the 6581 sound chip; their sound varies depending on the rising and falling of their output volume controlled by the wave envelope discussed later in the chapter.

TRIANGLE:

A very hollow or mellow sound, capable of producing the sound of an xylophone, chimes, flute and similar sounds.

SAWTOOTH:

A very twangy, brassy sound, capable of producing the sound of a harpsicord, trumpet and similar sounds.

PULSE:

A hollow to reedy sound, depending on the pulse width set (gap between each square wave), capable of producing a range of sounds from the piano to the clarinet.

NOISE:

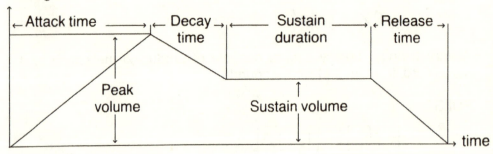

Noise, strangely enough, is a very versatile waveform used for producing sounds such as hissing, wind, the sea, gunshots, footsteps, clapping, a roaring crowd, etc.

THE ADSR ENVELOPE

The ADSR wave envelope is a device that gives us control over the rise and fall of the volume during sound output. ADSR stands for Attack/Decay/Sustain/Release. These are the four volume components of the envelope. The first stage of the ADSR envelope is the attack stage. The attack is actually the rate at which the volume is brought from zero level to peak volume. The peak (maximum) volume must be set before the envelope is used. A zero attack would give use an instantaneous output beginning at peak volume. A maximum attack setting (8 seconds of the 6581's envelope) would begin with zero volume and slowly increase volume until it reaches peak volume.

This brings us to the DECAY stage of the envelope. As soon as the volume reaches peak volume, the volume begins to decay (drop down) to the sustain volume at the set decay rate. As with the peak volume, the sustain level must be preset. The sustain level can be set to anywhere between 0 and peak volume. Once the volume has decayed down to the sustain level, the volume will stay at this level until a release signal is sent. On the 6581 a release signal is sent by setting the GATE bit to zero (see sound chip register map at the end of this chapter).

The release is just a secondary decay that decays the volume from the sustain level to zero volume at a rate determined by the decay rate setting.

With the general envelope, we can choose one of the four preset waveforms.

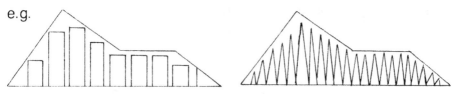

e.g.

and we can choose different frequencies (spacing between wave oscillations):

You can see that by using different combinations of waveforms and wave envelopes, it is possible to generate a large variety of sounds.

THE ADSR ENVELOPE

Summarizing the terms used to discuss the ADSR envelope.

ADSR   Attack/Decay/Sustain/Release envelope

ENVELOPE Shape of the volume of a sound over time

Attack   Rate at which a sound reaches peak volume

Decay   Rate at which a sound falls from peak volume to sustain volume

Sustain   The proportion of the peak volume that the volume will DECAY to

Release   Rate at which a sound falls from sustain volume to zero volume

Without the use of a wave envelope, it would be impossible to reproduce the sound of most of the existing musical instuments and the ability to produce complex sounds would be limited.

For example, in order to reproduce the sound of a violin you need the sound to build slowly, reach a peak then drop to a lower level and sustain, ie. for as long as desired after which the volume is allowed to slowly die away. This is similar to the ADSR envelope in the previous diagram. A table of the possible attack, decay and release times is as follows:

Value	Attack rate	Value	Decay/Release rate
0	2 ms	0	6 ms
16	8 ms	1	24 ms
32	16 ms	2	48 ms
48	24 ms	3	72 ms
64	38 ms	4	114 ms
80	56 ms	5	168 ms
96	68 ms	6	204 ms
112	80 ms	7	240 ms
128	100 ms	8	300 ms
144	250 ms	9	750 ms

Value	Attack rate	Value	Decay/Release rate
160	500 ms	10	1.5 s
176	800 ms	11	2.4 s
192	1 s	12	3 s
208	3 s	13	9 s
224	5 s	14	15 s
240	8 s	15	24 s

Later we will show how to use these values to control the ADSR envelope from a BASIC program.

CONTROLLING THE SOUND CHIP

Now that we know theoretically how to shape a sound to produce the sound we want, we can use the 6581 sound chip to put our knowledge into practice. The sound chip is controlled by changing values inside the sound chip's internal registers (memory cells within the sound chip). In order to control the sound chip via the computer, the sound chip registers have been memory mapped to the Commodore 64's memory. The memory used are locations 54272 to 54300. The sound chip is continually copying the values stored in the first 25 locations to the first 25 of its own respective registers. Thus, changing the contents of any of the locations 54272 to 54296 will have a direct effect on the operation of the sound chip. These memory locations are write-only, therefore no information can be obtained by reading them. Refer to the sound chip register map at the end of the chapter to see the significance of each sound chip register.

The first set of 7 registers make up the first sound channel or voice. There are three voices altogether, each as a whole, having the ability to generate a single sound. Each voice has frequency control, a choice of the four waveforms (previously discussed), an ADSR wave envelope and the ability to control the pulse width of the pulses. Other registers are used for filtering and peak-volume control. Finally, the last four registers are read-only registers used to store output from paddles, voice 3's waveform and voice 3's envelope.

PLAYING TUNES

The most practical way of writing a BASIC program to play a tune is to store the tune as data. For simple tunes, only two items of data are needed; the note frequency and the duration of each note to be played. The following steps are necessary when writing a BASIC program to play a simple tune.
1.   Simplify the addressing of all sound register memory locations to be used by assigning a variable name to each location.
2.   Clear the sound chip by setting all the sound chip registers to zero.

3.   POKE the attack/decay registers and the sustain/release registers with the attack, decay, release values chosen from the table in the envelope setting.

4.   Load the volume register with the maximum volume (ie. 15)

5.   Set up a program loop that does the following:

Read the frequency of the next note and the duration of the note. If there are no more frequencies then end. Otherwise, load the frequency registers with their data. Turn on the waveform and the GATE bit (see register map). Use a FOR NEXT loop to loop for the duration. Turn off the gate bit. Use a FOR NEXT loop to create a suitable pause (say 50 counts). Go back and do it again.

6.   Use the note table at the end of this chapter and durations using 1000 as an approximation of about 1 sec.

7.   End data with three negative values to signal end-of-tune.

Your program should look similar to the following:

```
5 REM * TUNE *
10 CHIP=54272 : C=CHIP
20 NL(0)=C+0:NH(0)=C+1:WK0)=C+4:AD(0)=C+5:SR(0)
   =C+6:VOLUME=C+24
30 FOR REG=CHIPTOCHIP+24:POKEREG,0:NEXT
40 POKE AD(0),64+9 : POKE SR(0),240+0
50 POKE VOLUME,15
60 READ F,DUR : IF F<0 THEN POKE WK0),0:END
65 DUR=DUR*20
70 NH(1)=INT(F/256):NL(1)=F-NH(1)*256:POKENH(0),
   NH(1):POKENL(0),NL(1)
80 POKE WK0),32+1:REM ADD 1 FOR GATE
90 FOR COUNT=1 TO DUR :NEXT COUNT
100 POKE WK0),32:REM TURN OFF GATE
110 FOR PAUSE=1 TO 50 :NEXT
120 GOTO 60
310 DATA 4820,8,6420,8,6420,12,6068,4,6420,8,
    8100,8,8100,8,7220,8,9637,8
320 DATA 9637,8,9637,12,8581,4,8100,8,7220,8,
    8100,16,4820,8,6420,8,6420,12
330 DATA 6068,4,6420,8,8100,8,8100,8,7220,8,
    9637,8,7220,8,7220,12,6068,4
340 DATA 6068,8,5396,8,4820,16
399 DATA -1,-1,-1
READY.
```

USING MULTIPLE VOICES

When using multiple voices you have the power to do many things not possible with a single voice. Some examples are orchestration, harmonization, special effects such as echo and other combinational sound effects.

In gaining these additional sound effects, it is necessary to include the programming complexity of timing. There are many methods in which to accomplish multiple voice programming, though the most effective method used so far is a method called the interpretive method. The simplified version of the interpretive method used here is as follows:

1. Simplify register addressing
2. For each voice:
Read note values and the duration of each note into arrays where a duration of 1 is a 1/16 beat and a zero for the high frequency signifies that the duration is a rest.
(The data may be a translation of a three-piece tune taken from sheet music.) If high is negative then store data count as end of tune for this voice.
3. Clear sound chip, set up ADSR values, waveforms for each voice and volume to 15, POKE in all values accept the waveform.
4. Initialize the note count array for each voice to zero.
5. The main loop should contain:
    a) Cycle through each voice (1 — 3)
    b) Test if duration of note for this voice has exhausted (i.e., less than 0) in which case increment the note counter and turn off the waveform.
    c) Insert a short pause to signify a breack between notes
    d) If high frequency $>$ 0 then turn on wave
    e) Load high and low note values into their registers.
    f) Decrement duration of note
    g) If end of tune for this voice then add one to end of tune counter
    h) If $E = 3$ then END
    i) Next voice
    j) Re-execute main loop

```
5 REM *** TUNES WITH MULTIPLE VOICES ***
10 CHIP=54272 : MAX=100
20 DIM F(13),H(3,MAX),L(3,MAX),D(3,MAX),W(3,1)
30 FORV=1TO3
40 C=CHIP+(V-1)*7
50 NL(V)=C+0:NH(V)=C+1:W(V,0)=C+4
60 NEXT V
65 FOR K=0 TO 13 : READ F(K) : NEXT
70 VOLUME=CHIP+24
80 FOR K=CHIPTOCHIP+24:POKEK,0
90 READ D:POKE K,D:NEXT
```

```
100 :
110 FORV=1TO3 : READ W(V,1)
120 N=1:N(V)=0
130 READ N$,D(V,N):IF N$="*"THEN E(V)=N:GOTO
    160
132 IF N$="-" THEN H(V,N)=0:GOTO 150
134 OC=VAL(RIGHT$(N$,1))
135 F=F((ASC(LEFT$(N$,1))-65)+(LEN(N$)-2)*7)
    *2↑OC+OC
140 H(V,N)=INT(F/256):L(V,N)=F-H(V,N)*256
150 N=N+1:GOTO 130
160 NEXT V
200 :
205 POKE VOLUME,7
210 FOR V=1TO3
220 D(V,N(V))=D(V,N(V))-1
230 IF D(V,N(V))<1THENN(V)=N(V)+1:POKEW(V,0)
    ,W(V,1)AND254:GOTO 280
240 H=H(V,N(V)):L=L(V,N(V))
250 IF H>0 THEN POKE W(V,0),W(V,1)
260 POKE NH(V),H:POKE NL(V),L
280 IF N(V)=E(V)THENE=E+1:POKEW(V,0),0:IF
    E=3THEN END
300 NEXT V
320 GOTO 210
800 REM NOTE-TABLE DATA
810 DATA 451,506,268,301,337,358,401,477,0,284
    ,318,0,379,425
900 REM SET-UP DATA (EDIT FOR FILTERS ETC.)
910 DATA 0,0,0,8,0,24,250
920 DATA 0,0,0,8,0,16,250
930 DATA 0,0,0,8,0,0,250
940 DATA 0,0,0,0
999 :
1000 DATA 65
1010 DATA D4,4,G4,4,G4,6,F#4,2
1020 DATA G4,4,B4,4,B4,4,A4,4
1030 DATA D5,4,D5,4,D5,6,C5,2
1040 DATA B4,4,A4,4,B4,8
1050 DATA D4,4,G4,4,G4,6,F#4,2
1060 DATA G4,4,B4,4,B4,4,A4,4
1070 DATA D5,4,A4,4,A4,6,F#4,2
```

57

```
1080 DATA F#4,4,E4,4,D4,8
1998 DATA *,0
1999 :
2000 DATA 33
2010 DATA D4,4,D4,4,D4,6,D4,2
2020 DATA D4,4,G4,4,G4,4,F#4,4
2030 DATA G4,4,F#4,4,E4,4,A4,4
2040 DATA G4,4,F#4,4,G4,8
2050 DATA D4,4,D4,4,D4,6,D4,2
2060 DATA E4,4,G4,4,G4,8
2070 DATA F#4,4,E4,4,F#4,6,D4,2
2080 DATA D4,4,C#4,4,D4,8
2998 DATA *,0
2999 :
3000 DATA 17
3010 DATA B3,4,B3,4,B3,6,A3,2
3020 DATA B3,4,D4,4,D4,8
3030 DATA D4,4,D4,4,C4,4,E4,4
3040 DATA D4,4,D4,4,D4,8
3050 DATA B3,4,B3,4,B3,6,A3,2
3060 DATA B3,4,D4,4,C#4,8
3070 DATA D4,4,E4,4,D4,6,A3,2
3080 DATA B3,4,G3,4,F#3,8
3999 DATA *,0
```

USING FILTERS AND RESONANCE

With the use of the 6581 sound filters and resonance, it is possible to generate exactly the sound you want by finding the appropriate basic waveform. Firstly, the three types of filters are Lowpass, Highpass and Bypass. There is a filter switch for each voice therefore giving you a choice of which voice(s) you wish to have filtered. There is also a filter switch for external sound input so that any sound device plugged into the audio/video socket will be filtered in the same way as sounds generated by the 6581.

HIGHPASS FILTER

The highpass filter will pass all frequencies at or above the cutoff frequency while attenuating the frequencies below the cutoff frequency.

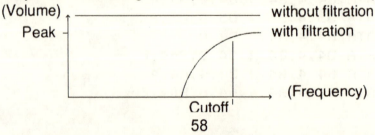

58

LOWPASS FILTER

The lowpass filter will pass all frequencies at or below the cutoff frequency while attenuating the frequencies above the cutoff frequency.

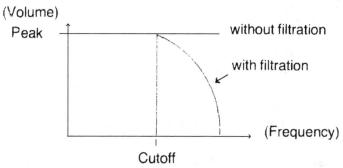

BANDPASS FILTER

The bandpass filter passes a narrow band of frequencies around the cutoff, and attenuates all others.

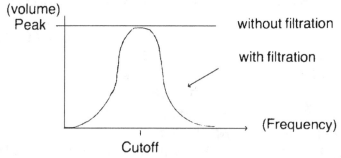

HIGH/LOW PASS COMBINATION

By combining the high and low pass filters it is possible to form what is called a notch reject filter which passes frequencies away from the cutoff frequency while attenuating at the cutoff frequency.

RESONANCE

Resonance has the effect of emphasizing a narrow band of frequencies around the cutoff point.

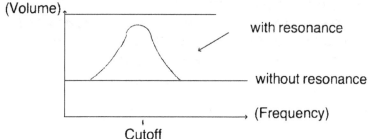

PUTTING IT ALL TOGETHER.

Now that you have convered all the basic operations of the 6581, it is time to put it to maximum use. The following program can be used to control all the features of the sound chip at the same time as giving you a visual representation exactly what is going on inside the chip including the shape of the ADSR envelope.

```
10 REM ***    SOUND GENERATOR    ***
15 DIM H(50),L(50),DU(50)
16 DIM NL(3,4),NH(3,4),PL(3,4),PH(3,4),WK(3,4),
   AD(3,4),SR(3,4):P$="O"
17 DV=.8:D(3)=DV*3/32:D(4)=DV*.5:D(5)=DV*1:D(6)
   =DV*.5                                    [25 CSRDWN]
20 Y$=" ▓▓▓▓▓▓▓▓▓▓▓▓▓▓▓▓▓▓▓▓▓▓▓▓▓▓":X$=  [40 CSRRT]
   "████████████████████████████████████████████"
21 S$="                                        "
22 DIM M1(14),M2(14),M3(14),M4(14)          [40 spaces]
25 DIMZ(14,5):FORR=1TO14:FORC=1TO5:READZ(R,C)
   :NEXT C,R
26 DATA2,25,0,3,2,3,25,0,15,1,3,25,0,240.16,3,
   25,0,15,1,3,25,0,240,16,3,25
27 DATA 0,15,1,1,25,0,32767,0,2,9,0,4,8,0,0,0,
   0,0,1,25,0,255,0,0,0,0,0,0,1,25
28 DATA 0,28,0,0,0,0,0,0,0,0,0,0,0
30 K=0:REM -READ TUNE DATA-
31 K=K+1:READ H(K),L(K),DU(K):IF H(K)<>-1THEN 31
32 ET=K-1
35 DATA 25,177,250,28,214,250,25,177,250,25,
   177,250,25,177,125,28,214,125
36 DATA32,94,750,25,177,250,28,214,250,19,63,
   250,19,63,250,19,63,250
37 DATA 21,154,63,24,63,63,25,177,250,24,63,
   125,19,63,250,-1,-1,-1
40 CHIP=54272:FORV=1TO3
41 C=CHIP+(V-1)*7:NL(V,0)=C+0:NH(V,0)=C+1
   :PL(V,0)=C+2:PH(V,0)=C+3:WK(V,0)=C+4
42 AD(V,0)=C+5:SR(V,0)=C+6:NEXT V
43 FL(0)=CHIP+21:FH(0)=CHIP+22:RF(0)=CHIP+23
   :MV(0)=CHIP+24
45 GOSUB50:GOSUB60:GOSUB1000:GOTO200
49 REM * CLEAR CHIP *
50 SWITCH=0:FOR S=CHIP TO CHIP+28:POKE
```

```
      S,0:NEXT:RETURN
 60   REM DISPLAY
 70   PRINT"◆▮▮";:POKE53281,0:POKE53280,4:REM
      BACKGROUND AND BORDER
 82   PRINT"A-VOICE(S)                    1 2 3
 83   PRINT"B-VOLUME   ───────0-15
 84   PRINT"C-ATTACK   ───────0-240
 85   PRINT"D-DECAY    ───────0-15
 86   PRINT"E-SUSTAIN ───────0-240
 87   PRINT"F-RELEASE ───────0-15
 88   PRINT"G-DURATION
 89   PRINT"H-WAVE 17=/\/ ,33=▬▮▮▮▮ ,65=⊓⎽⎽,
      129=NOISE
 90   PRINT"I-TEST NOTE
 91   PRINT"J-NOTE FREQ.    0-255
 93   PRINT"K-PLAY TUNE
 94   PRINT"L-LOAD A REGISTER
 95   PRINT"M-<SPARE OPTION>
 99   PRINT"N-EXIT PROGRAM
 100  GOSUB 1500
 110  PRINT"▮▮▮▮▮▮▮▮▮▮▮▮▮▮▮▮▮▮▮▮";
 111  PRINT"  ┌─────────────────────────────────────────────────────
 112  PRINT"A |                                                     |
 113  PRINT"M |                                                     |
 114  PRINT"P |                                                     |
 115  PRINT"L |                                                     |
 116  PRINT"I |                                                     |
 117  PRINT"T |                                                     |
 118  PRINT"U |                                                     |
 119  PRINT"D |                                                     |
 121  PRINT"E |                                                     |
 122  PRINT"  └ATTACK────DECAY────SUSTAIN────RELEASE─┘";
 190  GOSUB 1000
 199  RETURN
 200  REM * START *
 210  X=0:Y=0
 220  GET A$:Y=Y+1:IFY>13THENY=0
 222  IF A$=" "THENGOSUB50
 223  GOSUB500:PRINT"▮";CHR$(Y+65);:FORK=1TO10:
      NEXT
 225  PRINT"▮▮";CHR$(Y+65);"▮▮":IFA$<"A"ORA$>"N"
      THEN220
```

Annotation (line 89): Ctrl — 9 followed by three times Shift — £ and a Ctrl — 0

Annotation (line 110): HOME followed by 14 times CSRDWN

Annotation (line 225): CSRLFT followed by a CTRL — 0

61

```
230 R=ASC(A$)-64: X=0:Y=R-1:GOSUB500:
    PRINTCHR$(18);A$;
240 GOSUB 600:M1(R)=M(1):M2(R)=M(2):M3(R)=M(3)
    :M4(R)=M(4)
245 IF R>1ANDR<7THEN:M=R:GOSUB1000:R=M
250 ONRGOSUB310,320,330,340,350,360,370,380,
    390,400,410,420,430,440
253 IF(R=8ANDW=65)THENGOSUB110
254 IF Z(R,1)<>0THENGOSUB2000
255 X=0:Y=R-1:GOSUB500:PRINT"█";CHR$(Y+65);
260 GOTO 200
300 REM * OPTION DEPENDANT ROUTINES *
303 REM * VALUES FROM INPUT ROUTINE *
304 REM * HELD IN:                  *
305 REM * M1(R),M2(R),M3(R),M4(R)   *
306 REM * WHERE R IS THE OPTION ROW *
307 REM * (IE. C-ATTACK IS ROW 3)   *
309 REM *****************************
310 REM -VOICE(S)-
312 V(1)=M1(R):V(2)=M2(R):V(3)=M3(R)
319 RETURN
320 REM -VOLUME-
322 MV(1)=M1(R)
329 RETURN
330 REM -ATTACK-
332 FOR V=1 TO 3:AD(V,1)=M1(R):NEXT
339 RETURN
340 REM -DECAY-
342 FOR V=1 TO 3:AD(V,2)=M1(R):NEXT
349 RETURN
350 REM -SUSTAIN-
352 FOR V=1 TO 3:SR(V,1)=M1(R):NEXT V
359 RETURN
360 REM -RELEASE-
362 FOR V=1 TO 3:SR(V,2)=M1(R):NEXT
369 RETURN
370 REM -DURATION-
372 DUR=M1(R)
379 RETURN
380 REM -WAVE-
381 IF M3(R)=1THENFORV=1TO3:PH(V,1)=M1(R)
    :PL(V,1)=M2(R):NEXT V:M1(R)=0:M2(R)=0
```

62

```
382 IF M1(R)=1THENW=17
383 IF M2(R)=1THENW=33
384 IF M3(R)=1THENW=65
385 IF M4(R)=1THENW=129
388 FOR V=1 TO 3:W(V,1)=W:NEXT
389 RETURN
390 REM -TEST NOTE-
391 IF SWITCH=0 THEN GOSUB 2000
394 FOR V=1 TO 3:POKE W(V,0),W(V,1):NEXT
396 FOR T=1TODUR:NEXT
397 IF PEEK(197)=33THEN397
398 FORV=1TO3:POKEW(V,0),W(V,1)AND254:NEXT
399 RETURN
400 REM -NOTE FREQ.-
402 FOR V=1TO3 :NH(V,1)=M1(R):NL(V,1)=M2(R):NEXT
409 RETURN
410 REM -PLAY TUNE-
412 GOSUB50:IF SWITCH=0 THEN GOSUB2000
413 FORK=1TOET
414 FORV=1TO3:IFV(V)=1THENPOKENH(V,0),H(K)
    :POKENL(V,0),L(K):POKEW(V,0),W(V,1)
415 NEXTV:FOR T=1TODUR:IFPEEK(197)=64THEN
    T=DUR:K=ET
417 NEXT T:FORV=1TO3:POKEW(V,0),W(V,1)AND254
    :NEXT V,K
418 IF PEEK(197)<>64THEN413
419 GOSUB 2000:RETURN
420 REM -LOAD A SID REGISTER-
422 POKE CHIP+M1(R),M2(R)
429 RETURN
430 REM -SPARE OPTION-
439 RETURN
440 REM -EXIT-
442 GOSUB 50
444 PRINT"░░░CONT:HIT RETURN TO
    CONTINUE████░░░";:END
459 GOTO45
499 STOP
500 REM * PRINT-AT ROUTINE *
510 PRINT"░";::IFX>0THENPRINTLEFT$(X$,X);
520 IFY>0THENPRINTLEFT$(Y$,Y);
530 RETURN
```

[Note at line 442:] CLR followed by 2 times CSRDWN

[Note at line 459:] CSRLEFT times 3 and 3 times CSRUP

```
600 REM *** INPUT ROUTINES ***
603 IF Z(R,1)=0THENRETURN
604 FORK=1TO4:M(K)=0:NEXT
605 X=Z(R,2):Y=R-1:L=Z(R,3):U=Z(R,4):
    INC=Z(R,5):M=0:K=0:P=1024+X+Y*40
610 ON Z(R,1) GOTO 620,700,800
620 REM -USING INPUT?-
625 IF R<>8ANDR<>10ANDR<>12ANDR<>13THENHL$=""
    :GOTO630
626 IF M=0ANDR<>12THENHL$="HIGH":GOTO630
627 IF M=0ANDR=12THENHL$="REGISTER": GOTO630
628 IFR=12THENHL$="VALUE":U=255:GOTO630
629 HL$="LOW"
630 GOSUB500:PRINT"█";LEFT$(S$,39-POS(0));
    :GOSUB500:PRINTHL$;:INPUTI$:I=VAL(I$)
640 GOSUB500:PRINT"█           ";
645 IFI<LORI>UTHEN620                    ┌─ CTRL-9
650 GOSUB500:PRINT"◤";:IF M=1THENPRINTSTR$(M(1));
    STR$(I);" █         ";:GOTO660
655 PRINTRIGHT$(STR$(I),LEN(STR$(I))-1);
660 M(M+1)=I:IF(R=8ORR=100RR=120RR=13)
    ANDM=0THENM=1:GOTO620
670 RETURN
675 REM -SET PULSE FREQ.-
680 GOSUB 1100:X=5:Y=20:L=0:U=255:GOSUB500:
    PRINT"PULSE FREQUENCY";:X=25:GOTO620
700 REM -CHOICE-
705 FOROFF=XTOINC*(U-1)+XSTEP INC:POKE1024+OFF
    +Y*40,PEEK(1024+OFF+Y*40)AND127
706 NEXT OFF:K=0
710 GOSUB500:POKEP,PEEK(P)AND127:FORT=1TO50:
    NEXT:POKEP,PEEK(P)OR128
720 GET B$:IFB$="█"THENK=K+1:POKEP,PEEK(P)AND
    127:GOTO750
730 IFB$<>CHR$(13)THEN710
740 K=K+1:M(K)=1
745 IF R=8 THEN 770
750 IF K=U THEN 770
760 X=X+INC : P=P+INC : GOTO 710
770 IF R=8ANDK=3THEN 675
790 RETURN
800 REM -INPUT USING UP & DOWN CURSOR-
```

```
801 GOSUB802:GOTO805
802 REM
303 B(3)=M1(3)*D(3):B(4)=M1(4)*D(4):B(6)=M1(6)
    *D(6)
804 B=-B(3)*(R>3)-B(4)*(R>4)-4*(R>5)-B(6)*(R>6)
    +2:NY=23-M1(2)/2:NX=39:RETURN
805 FOR Z=1TO4:M(Z)=0:NEXT
810 GOSUB500 : M=M1(R)
820 GOSUB500:PRINT"██▜";M;"██           ";
824 GOSUB500:PRINT"██ ";:GETB$
825 IFB$=CHR$(13)THENM(1)=M:X=NX:Y=NY:
    GOSUB500:PRINT" ";:RETURN
827 GOSUB 900
830 IF B$<>"□"THEN860
840 M=M+INC:IFM>UTHENM=L
850 GOSUB 900:GOTO820
860 IF B$<>"█"THEN820
870 M=M-INC:IFM<LTHENM=U
880 GOSUB 900:GOTO 820
900 REM *** MOVE ENVELOPE CURSOR ***
910 IF R<3 OR R=5 OR R>6 THEN RETURN
920 MX=X:MY=Y:X=NX:Y=NY:GOSUB500:PRINT" ";
930 X=B+M*D(R):Y=NY:GOSUB 500:PRINT"+";:NX=X:
    NY=Y:X=MX:Y=MY
999 RETURN
1000 REM *** UPDATE ADSR DISPLAY ***
1010 GOSUB 1100
1020 X=2:Y=23:GOSUB 500:PRINT"o";
1030 R=3:GOSUB802:X=B+M1(R)*D(R):Y=NY:GOSUB
     500:PRINT"A";
1040 R=4:GOSUB802:X=B+M1(R)*D(R):Y=23-(M1(2)
     *M1(5)/240)/2:GOSUB 500:PRINT"D-S-";
1060 R=6:GOSUB802:X=B+M1(R)*D(R):Y=23:GOSUB
     500:PRINT"R";
1099 RETURN
1100 REM * CLEAR ADSR DISPLAY *
1120 X=2:FORY=15TO23:GOSUB500:PRINT"█";
     LEFT$(S$,35);:NEXT
1139 RETURN
1200 REM * PLOTTER *
1220 X=X2:Y=Y2:GOSUB500:PRINTP$;
1299 RETURN
```

CSRLFT followed by CTRL — 9

CSRDWN

```
1500 REM * UPDATE PARAMETER DISPLAY *
1520 FOR R=1 TO 14:IF Z(R,1)=0THEN1540
1525 X=Z(R,2):Y=R-1:L=Z(R,3):U=Z(R,4):INC=Z(R,5)
1530 ON Z(R,1)GOSUB 1600,1700,1800
1540 NEXT R
1550 RETURN
1600 REM -1-
1610 IF R=100RR=13THENGOSUB500:PRINT"█";
     STR$(M1(R));STR$(M2(R));" ■";:GOTO1699
1620 GOSUB500:PRINT"██";M1(R);:GOSUB 500:
     PRINT"██ ";
1699 RETURN
1700 REM -2-
1710 K=0:FORZ=XTOINC*(U-1)+XSTEPINC
1720 P=1024+Z+Y*40:K=K+1
1730 M=-M1(R)*(K=1)-M2(R)*(K=2)-M3(R)*(K=3)
     -M4(R)*(K=4)
1740 IFM=1THENPOKE P,PEEK(P)OR128:GOTO 1790
1750 POKE P,PEEK(P)AND127
1790 NEXTZ
1799 RETURN
1800 REM -3-
1820 GOTO1600
1899 RETURN
2000 REM * LOAD CHIP WITH VALUES SET *
2001 REM * FROM OPTION LIST.          *
2030 FOR V=1 TO 3
2040 IF V(V)=0THENPOKEW(V,0),0:GOTO2190
2100 POKE NL(V,0),NL(V,1)
2110 POKE NH(V,0),NH(V,1)
2120 POKE PL(V,0),PL(V,1)
2130 POKE PH(V,0),PH(V,1)
2140 POKE  W(V,0), W(V,1)AND254
2150 POKE AD(V,0),AD(V,1)+AD(V,2)
2160 POKE SR(V,0),SR(V,1)+SR(V,2)
2190 NEXT V
2240 POKE MV(0),MV(1)
2298 SWITCH=1
2299 RETURN
```

CTRL—9 (annotation pointing to line 1610)

CSRLFT and a CTRL—9 (annotation pointing to line 1620)

SPECIAL SOUND EFFECTS

Apart from generating sound by presetting the sound chip and controlling the sound via the ADSR envelope, some interesting sound effects can be produced by dynamically controlling various features of the sound chip during sound output.

LINKING REGISTERS

An effective way to dynamically control sound during output is to link the output from the envelope or waveform of one voice to one of the registers of another voice. To do this in BASIC you would need to continually PEEK one of the output registers (25 — 28) and POKE this value to the register representing the feature you wish to control. However, using BASIC would produce a staggered sound movement owing to BASIC's speed inefficiency compared to the speed of the sound chip's waveform oscillation. To produce smooth sound changes, you need a machine language routine to link the registers at high speed (preferably independent of your program). The following program "REGLINK" will suit this pupose.

```
0 GOTO 10 :      *** REGLINK ***
5 *** POKE 820-823 WITH DESTINATION
  REGISTER TO BE
6 *** LINKED TO SOUND REGISTERS 25-28
  RESPECTIVELY
7 :
10 FOR I=0TO16:READ A:POKE49152+I,A:NEXT
20 POKE 56333,127
30 POKE 788,0 :POKE 789,192
40 POKE 56333,129
100 DATA 160,3,185,25,212,190,52,3,157,0
110 DATA 212
120 DATA 136,16,244,76,49,234
```

The BASIC program will wedge the M/L (machine language) program into the operating system so as not to effect BASIC. We will use this program in the vibrato example on the next page. To use the routine use the following format:
POKE [820 — 823], [any sound chip register]
where locations 820 — 823 are mapped to sound chip registers 25 — 28 respectively (see register map).

Even within BASIC programming, it is possible to generate some quite interesting effects, such as echo, vibrato, modulation, portamento and many others.

ECHO

There are many methods by which to accomplish this effect. One method is to generate a sound with a sharp attack, medium decay and low sustain level, then replaying the sound by turning off the wave and turning it on again with a lower volume setting and repeating this until either a zero volume has been reached or another sound is played.

```
10 CHIP = 54272 : VOLUME = CHIP + 24
20 POKE CHIP + 5, 16 + 3 : POKE CHIP + 6, 0 + 0
30 V = 15 : POKE VOLUME, V
40 POKE CHIP + 1, 10
50 FOR ECHO = 1 TO 7
60 POKE CHIP + 4, 17
70 FOR COUNT = 1 TO 100 : NEXT COUNT
80 POKE CHIP + 4, 0 : REM TURN OFF WAVEFORM
90 V = V * 0.6 : POKE VOLUME, V : NEXT ECHO
100 FOR I = 1 TO 500 : NEXT : GOTO 30
```

VIBRATO: (A rapid variation in frequency)

This effect is accomplished by copying the output of voice 3's oscillator (register 27) to the input of the low note frequency of the voice(s) you wish to effect. When using this method, the vibrato will be controlled by voice 3, therefore voice 3 must be operating, preferably with the triangle waveform and the output turned off (to turn voice -3 output off, set bit 7 of register 24 to 1). If 'REGLINK' has been loaded then adding the following lines to the end of the initialization section of any Sound program will give the vibrato effect to each note played.

POKE CHIP + 15, 10 : POKE CHIP + 18, 17 : POKE CHIP + 24, 128 + volume setting
POKE 822, 0 : POKE 823, 28
where the vibrato speed is controlled by the frequency setting of voice 3.

MODULATION: (A continued variation in volume)

This effect is accomplished in much the same way as vibrato except that voice 3's oscillator (register 27) is linked to the master volume control. Also, the fact that register 27 outputs from 0 to 15 means that the output from register 27 must first be divided by 17. The BASIC statement to link the two registers (for voice 1) is as follows:
POKE CHIP + 24, PEEK (CHIP + 27)/ 17
where CHIP = 54272

In this case 'REGLINK' cannot be used owing to the fact that volume requires values 0 — 15 whereas a direct linkage would give values 0 — 255. Therefore the above BASIC statement must be executed as often as possible to produce the desired effect.

The following program demonstrates modulation:

```
10 CHIP = 54272
20 POKE CHIP + 1, 30 : REM NOTE FREQUENCY
30 POKE CHIP + 6, 240 : REM MAX SUSTAIN
40 POKE CHIP + 15, 10 : REM MODULATION SPEED
50 POKE CHIP + 18, 17 : REM TRIANGLE WAVE (VOICE 3)
60 POKE CHIP + 24, 128 : REM TURN OFF VOICE 3 OUTPUT
* continual link of waveform to volume *
70 POKE CHIP + 24, PEEK (CHIP + 27) / 17 + 128 : GOTO 70
```

Run the above program and edit line 40 to obtain different modulation speeds.

PORTAMENTO: (Frequency slide)

The portamento is a gradual slide from one frequency to another. It can be used to simulate an accellerating jet, a falling bomb or it can be used in music to create a sliding instrument such as a trombone. This effect is accomplished by incrementing/decrementing the frequency of the last note played to the frequency of the next note played. Your portamento subroutine should look somethng like this:

```
1000 INC = SGN (NF – OF)
1010 OF = OF + INC
1020 POKE CHIP + 1, OF
1030 IF OF  <  NF THEN 1000
1040 RETURN
where   CHIP = 54272
        OF = high frequency of old note
        NF = high frequency of next note
```

THE SOUND CHIP REGISTERS

Bit significance

Register usage
(Voice-1)

REG No.	b7	b6	b5	b4	b3	b2	b1	b0	
0	NL_7	NL_6	NL_5	NL_4	NL_3	NL_2	NL_1	NL_0	Low byte of note frequency
1	NH_7	NH_6	NH_5	NH_4	NH_3	NH_2	NH_1	NH_0	High byte of note frequency
2	PL_7	PL_6	PL_5	PL_4	PL_3	PL_2	PL_1	PL_0	Low byte of pulse width
3	—	—	—	—	PH_3	PH_2	PH_1	PH_0	High byte of pulse width
4	Noise	⊓⊔	/\\/\\	/\\	TEST	RING MOD	SYNC	GATE	Wave form control
5	A_3	A_2	A_1	A_0	D_3	D_2	D_1	D_0	Attack/decay for envelope
6	S_3	S_2	S_1	S_0	R_3	R_2	R_1	R_0	Sustain/release for envelope

Voices 2 and 3 are mirror images of the above except that they are stored in registers 7 to 13 and 14 to 20 respectively.

Bit significance

Register usage
(Filter)

	b7	b6	b5	b4	b3	b2	b1	b0	
21	—	—	—	—	—	CL_2	CL_1	CL_0	Low cutoff frequency
22	CH_7	CH_6	CH_5	CH_4	CH_3	CH_2	CH_1	CH_0	High cutoff frequency
23	R_3	R_2	R_1	R_0	F_{EX}	F_3	F_2	F_1	Filter switches and resonance
24	3_{OFF}	HP	BP	LP	V_3	V_2	V_1	V_0	Filter modes and volume

Bit significance

Register usage
(Misc.)

	b7	b6	b5	b4	b3	b2	b1	b0	
25	P_7	P_6	P_5	P_4	P_3	P_2	P_1	P_0	Paddle - x
26	P_7	P_6	P_5	P_4	P_3	P_2	P_1	P_0	Paddle - y
27	O_7	O_6	O_5	O_4	O_3	O_2	O_1	O_0	Oscillator - 3 output
28	E_7	E_6	E_5	E_4	E_3	E_2	E_1	E_0	Envelope - 3 output

NOTE: The sound chip registers are accessed via memory locations 54272 to 54300.

REGISTERS 0 AND 1 (Location 54272 and 54273)

(Low and high bytes of note frequency)
These two registers form a two byte value corresponding to the frequency of a note played. To obtain the actual frequency of the note being played multiply the two byte value by 0.059604645.

REGISTERS 2 AND 3 (Location 54274 and 54275)

(Low and high bytes of pulse width of pulse wave)
These two registers form a 12-bit value corresponding to the pulse width of the pulse wave. The width of the low pulse of the pulse cycle as a percentage of the width of the pulse cycle is given by the following formula:
Low pulse width = (12-bit value/40.95)% of the pulse cycle. Where a low pulse width of 0% or 100% is a constant DC signal (i.e. zero output) and a low pulse width of 50% is a square wave.

REGISTER 4 (Location 54276)

(Waveform control)
This register serves several functions where each bit serves a seperate function.

Bit 0 (Gate Bit):
The gate bit controls the envelope generator. Setting this bit to a 1 turns on the ADSR envelope and begins the envelope cycle at the attack stage, goes on to the decay stage and finally the sustain. The sound will continue at the sustain level until the gate bit is set to zero, in which case envelope control will continue to the release stage. If the gate bit is set to zero before the sustain stage has been reached then envelope control will jump to the release stage.

Bit-1 (Sync Bit):
Setting the sync bit to 1 causes the waveform from voice 3 to be syncronized with voice 1. Varying the frequency of voice 3 will change the overall waveform output of voice 1.

Bit-2 (Ring Mod Bit):
Setting the ring mod bit to a 1 replaces the triangle waveform of voice 1 with a 'ring-modulated' combination of oscillators 1 and 3 for giving the output a bell type sound. Varying the frequency of oscillator 3 causes changes in the overall waveform output of voice 1.

Bit-3 (Test Bit):
Mainly used for testing, this bit when set to 1, causes oscillator 1 to reset to 0 and lock there until the bit is reset. However, it can be used to synchronize oscillator 1 to an external device.

Bit-4 (Triangle Waveform):
When set to 1, this bit selects the triangle waveform to be used for output of oscillator 1.

Bit-5 (Sawtooth Waveform):
When set to 1, this bit selects the sawtooth waveform.

Bit-6 (Pulse Waveform):
When set to 1, selects the pulse waveform.

Bit-7 (Noise Waveform):
When set to 1, selects the noise waveform.

REGISTER 5 (Location 54277)

(Attack/decay)
This register is used to select the attack and decay rate for voice 1's ADSR envelope.

Bits 4 — 7 (Attack Rate):
Selects an attack rate from 0 — 240 where the attack times range from 2ms to 8s.

Bits 0 — 3 (Decay Rate):
Select a decay rate from 0 — 15 where the decay times range from 6ms to 24s.

REGISTER 6 (Location 54278)

(Sustain/release)
This register is used to select the sustain level and release rate for voice 1's ADSR envelope.

Bits 4 — 7 (Sustain Rate):
Selects a sustain level from 0 — 240 where the sustain setting is a proportion of the volume setting. To obtain the actual sustain volume use the following equation:
Sustain volume = (volume setting *sustain setting) / 240

Bits 0 — 3 (Release Rate):
Selects a release rate from 0 — 15 where the release times range from 6ms to 24s.

REGISTERS 7 — 13 (Locations 54279 — 54285)

(Voice 2)
These registers are functionally identical to registers 0 — 6 (voice 1) with the following exceptions:
1.   SYNC — Synchronizes oscillator 2 with oscillator 1.

2.   RING MOD — Replaces the triangle output of oscillator 2 with the ring modulated combination of oscillators 2 and 1.

REGISTERS 14 — 20 (Locations 54286 — 54292)

(Voice 3)

These registers are functionally identical to registers 0 — 6 (voice 1) and registers 7 — 13 (voice 2) with the following exceptions:

1.   SYNC — Syncronizes oscillator 3 with oscillator 2.

2.   RING MOD — Replaces the triangle output of oscillator 3 with the ring modulated combination of oscillators 3 and 2.

REGISTERS 21 AND 22 (Locations 54293 and 54294)

(Cutoff frequency)

These two registers form an 11-bit value corresponding to the cutoff (or centre) frequency of the programmable filter. They select a cutoff value of 0 — 262 where the cutoff frequency ranges from 30 Hz — 12KHz.

REGISTER 23 (Location 54295)

(Resonance/filter)

This register is used to select the resonance and filter switches.

Bit-0 (Filter Switch 1):

When set to 1, voice 1 is sent through the filters before output. When set to 0, voice 1 is sent directly to output.

Bits 1 and 2 (Filter Switches 2 and 3):

Same as bit 0 but for voices 2 and 3 respectively.

Bit-3 (Filter Switch EXT):

Same as bit 0 but for external audio input.

Bits 4 — 7 (Resonance Setting):

This register forms a 4-bit value corresponding to the resonance setting of the programmable filter. They select resonance settings that range from 16 — 240 in steps of 16. The resonance acts on a small band of frequencies around the selected cutoff frequency.

REGISTER 24 (Location 54296)

(Voice 3's switch/filter modes/volume setting)

Bits 0 — 3 (Volume Setting):

These four bits are used to select volume settings which range from 0 — 15. This is a master volume control, however each voice may be varied

73

by either setting a large attack and setting the gate bit to 0 during attack or by setting a different sustain level for each voice, thus achieving different volume levels for each voice within the absolute level set by the above four bits.

Bits 4 — 6 (Filter Modes):
These three bits are used to select the filter modes for the programmable filter. Bit 5 selects the 'lowpass' filter, bit 6 selects the 'bandpass' filter and bit 7 selects the 'highpass' filter. More than one filter may be selected at one time. For example, a 'notch reject' filter can be set up by selecting the lowpass and highpass filters.

Bit-7 (Voice 3 Switch):
Setting this bit to 1 causes voice 3 output to be disconnected without effecting any of the voice 3 controls. This switch is used when voice 3 is used to control another voice and the output of voice 3 is not needed.

REGISTERS 25 AND 26 (Location 54297 and 54298)

(Paddles)
These registers allow the microprocessor to read the positions of a pair of paddles conected to port-1 (labelled port-2 on computer casing). The paddles should give readings of 0 for minimum resistance and 255 for maximum resistance. By reading these registers and writing their contents to other sound chip registers, it is possible to control the sound chip with the paddles.

REGISTER 27 (Location 54299)

(Oscillator 3 output)
This register allows the microprocessor to read the waveform output of voice 3 where any waveform will produce values between 0 and 255. For example, if the sawtooth is selected, register 27 will output incrementing values from 0 to 255 at a rate depending on the frequency setting of voice 3.

REGISTER 28 (Location 54300)

(Envelope 3 output)
Same as register 27, but this register allows the microprocessor to read the envelope output of voice 3.

MUSIC NOTE VALUES

This appendix contains a complete list of Note#, actual note, and the values to be POKEd into the HI FREQ and LOW FREQ registers of the sound chip to produce the indicated note.

MUSICAL NOTE		OSCILLATOR FREQ		
NOTE	OCTAVE	DECIMAL	HI	LOW
0	C–0	268	1	12
1	C#–0	284	1	28
2	D–0	301	1	45
3	D#–0	318	1	62
4	E–0	337	1	81
5	F–0	358	1	102
6	F#–0	379	1	123
7	G–0	401	1	145
8	G#–0	425	1	169
9	A–0	451	1	195
10	A#–0	477	1	221
11	B–0	506	1	250
16	C–1	536	2	24
17	C#–1	568	2	56
18	D–1	602	2	90
19	D#–1	637	2	125
20	E–1	675	2	163
21	F–1	716	2	204
22	F#–1	758	2	246
23	G–1	803	3	35

MUSICAL NOTE		OSCILLATOR FREQ		
NOTE	OCTAVE	DECIMAL	HI	LOW
24	G#-1	851	3	83
25	A-1	902	3	134
26	A#-1	955	3	187
27	B-1	1012	3	244
32	C-2	1072	4	48
33	C#-2	1136	4	112
34	D-2	1204	4	180
35	D#-2	1275	4	251
36	E-2	1351	5	71
37	F-2	1432	5	152
38	F#-2	1517	5	237
39	G-2	1607	6	71
40	G#-2	1703	6	167
41	A-2	1804	7	12
42	A#-2	1911	7	119
43	B-2	2025	7	233
48	C-3	2145	8	97
49	C#-3	2273	8	225
50	D-3	2408	9	104
51	D#-3	2551	9	247
52	E-3	2703	10	143
53	F-3	2864	11	48
54	F#-3	3034	11	218
55	G-3	3215	12	143
56	G#-3	3406	13	78
57	A-3	3608	14	24
58	A#-3	3823	14	239
59	B-3	4050	15	210
64	C-4	4291	16	195
65	C#-4	4547	17	195
66	D-4	4817	18	209
67	D#-4	5103	19	239
68	E-4	5407	21	31
69	F-4	5728	22	96
70	F#-4	6069	23	181
71	G-4	6430	25	30
72	G#-4	6812	26	156
73	A-4	7217	28	49

MUSICAL NOTE		OSCILLATOR FREQ		
NOTE	OCTAVE	DECIMAL	HI	LOW
74	A# – 4	7647	29	223
75	B – 4	8101	31	165
80	C – 5	8583	33	135
81	C# – 5	9094	35	134
82	C – 0	9634	37	162
83	C# – 0	10207	39	223
84	D – 0	10814	42	62
85	F – 5	11457	44	193
86	F# – 5	12139	47	107
87	G – 5	12860	50	60
88	G# – 5	13625	53	57
89	A – 5	14435	56	99
90	A# – 5	15294	59	190
91	B – 5	16203	63	75
96	C – 6	17167	67	15
97	C# – 6	18188	71	12
98	D – 6	19269	75	69
99	D# – 6	20415	79	191
100	E – 6	21629	84	125
101	F – 6	22915	89	131
102	F# – 6	24278	94	214
103	G – 6	25721	100	121
104	G# – 6	27251	106	115
105	A – 6	28871	112	199
106	A# – 6	30588	119	124
107	B – 6	32407	126	151
112	C – 7	34334	134	30
113	C# – 7	36376	142	24
114	D – 7	38539	150	139
115	D# – 7	40830	159	126
116	E – 7	43258	168	250
117	F – 7	45830	179	6
118	F# – 7	48556	189	172
119	G – 7	51443	200	243
120	G# – 7	54502	212	230
121	A – 7	57743	225	143
122	A# – 7	61176	238	248
123	B – 7	64814	253	46

FILTER SETTINGS

Location	Contents
54293	Low cutoff frequency (0−7)
54294	High cutoff frequency (0−255)
54295	Resonance (bits 4−7) Filter voice 3 (bit 2) Filter voice 2 (bit 1) Filter voice 1 (bit 0)
54296	High pass (bit 6) Bandpass (bit 5) Low pass (bit 4) Volume (bits 0−3)

CHAPTER 5

GRAPHICS

As you probably already know, the Commodore 64 has graphics capabilities available directly from the keyboard, using the graphics characters, colour control keys, cursor control keys and PRINT statements. However, it also has more powerful graphics capabilities available through direct user control of sections of the memory.

Graphics Memory

There are three blocks of memory used to control graphics on the Commodore 64 — screen memory, colour memory and character memory — and a few odd bytes we'll discuss as we get to them. First, a brief description of the three blocks, then a more detailed coverage of how to use them.

Screen memory consists of one byte for each character position on the screen. Since the screen has 1000 character positions — 25 rows of 40 characters — screen memory has 1000 bytes. The first 40 bytes of screen memory correspond to the first row on the screen, the second 40 bytes correspond to the second row, and so on.

Colour memory, like screen memory, consists of 1 byte for each screen character position. Each byte contains a code for the colour in which characters will be displayed at that position.

Character memory contains the coded representations of all printable characters. It is broken into 2 blocks — one for upper case and graphics characters, the other for lower and upper case characters.

To display a character on the screen, the Commodore 64 finds the code for the character in screen memory, uses the code as a pointer to the character representation in character memory, finds the colour of the character position in colour memory and uses all this information to display the character.

LOW RESOLUTION GRAPHICS

Screen Background and Border Colours.

These colours are controlled by the value in locations 53280 and 53281. The values for background/border colour combinations are given in Appendix I.

e.g. POKE 53280, 7 : POKE 53281, 4 gives a yellow border around a purple screen.

Character Colour
Keyboard Control
As previously mentioned, the colour of characters can be dictated using the colour control keys. These keys can be included in strings within a program. They change the value in byte 646. This value can also be changed by POKEing.

Changing this value causes everything after the change to be printed in the colour set, i.e. it changes character colour from then on. From this it follows that you must change this value every time you want to change character colour just as you do when using the colour control keys.

Colour Memory Control
Colour memory uses locations 55296 to 56319. You can POKE values into colour memory thus controlling the colour of individual character positions on the screen. This determines the colour of characters POKEd into screen memory, but not characters which are PRINTed. These are controlled by byte 646.

You may now determine the colour of characters POKEd into screen memory by POKEing the desired values into the relevant bytes of colour memory.

0	Black	4	Purple	8	Orange	12	Grey 2
1	White	5	Green	9	Brown	13	Light Green
2	Red	6	Blue	10	Light Red	14	Light Blue
3	Cyan	7	Yellow	11	Grey 1	15	Grey 3

e.g.   10 CM = 55296
       20 FOR J = CM TO CM + 1000
       30 POKE J, 7 : NEXT

Screen Memory
The default position of screen memory is at 1024. Screen memory can be moved to any location that is a multiple of 1024 as long as it doesn't sit on top of other memory locations such as your BASIC program.
Byte 648 contains the number of ¼K bytes from 0 to screen memory address. Byte 53272 contains the number of K bytes from 0 to screen memory address. Byte 648 is a pointer for the screen editor. Byte 53272 is the actual pointer.

The simple way to calculate the address of the bytes in screen memory you want to POKE is to use the formula – SM + (row*22) + column. Where SM is the start of screen memory, 'row' is the screen row number (0 is the top row) and 'column' is how far along the row (also starting from 0 at the left of the screen).

Graph paper is handy for working out screen displays.

The values POKEd into screen memory act as pointers into character memory. The are NOT the ASCII values of the characters. The screen codes corresponding to ASCII values are shown below:

ASCII value	Screen value
0-31	None – not displayable
32-63	32-63
64-95	0-31
96-127	64-95
128-159	None – not displayable
160-191	96-127
192-254	64-126
255	94

You will notice that some screen codes are shared by two ASCII codes. This is because character memory is broken into two blocks. The character displayed by a screen code corresponding to two ASCII codes will depend on which block of characters is being used. The screen code, as was mentioned, acts as a pointer into the block of character memory. (see Character Memory section for more details.)

A table of ASCII and screen codes for the two character sets is given in Appendix A. When you know in advance what characters are to be POKEd into screen memory, this table may be used to look up the screen values. However, for some applications, such as GETting characters from the keyboard, the characters can not be known in advance. The ASCII codes convert in blocks of 32 so the screen codes may be calculated using the following subroutine:

```
 10  GET K$
 20  SC = ASC (K$)
 30  ON INT (SC/32) +1 GOTO 40 , 50 , 60 , 70 , 80 , 90 , 100
 40  SC = -1 : RETURN
 50  RETURN
 60  SC = SC-64 : RETURN
 70  SC = SC-32 : RETURN
 80  SC = -1 : RETURN
 90  SC = SC-64 : RETURN
100  IF SC = 255 THEN SC = 94 : RETURN
101  SC = SC-128 : RETURN
```

This subroutine returns −1 when the character is not displayable. The main program can then decide what to do with it.

The following example program POKEs red 'A's into the top half of the screen, green 'Z's into the bottom half:

```
10  REM Set up colour memory
20  CM = 55296
30  REM Red character positions
40  FOR J = 0 TO 499
50  POKE CM + J , 2 : NEXT
60  REM Green character positions
70  FOR J = 500 TO 1000
80  POKE CM + J , 5 : NEXT
90  SM = 256 * PEEK (648)
100 REM Poke A's into first half of screen memory
110 FORJ= 0 TO 499
120 POKE SM + J , 1 : NEXT
130 REM Poke Z's into second half
140 FORJ = 500 TO 999
150 POKE SM + J , 26 : NEXT
160 GOTO 160 : REM Wait for STOP keystroke
```

Character Memory

Before going into the Commodore 64's character memory it would be worthwhile to first have a look at the character table and then follow this with the memory and how to use it in designing your own characters.

The first block of character memory — upper case, graphics, reversed upper case, and reversed graphics occupies the ROM locatons 53248 — 55295. The second block — lower case, upper case, reversed lower case, reversed upper case and graphics — occupies ROM locations 55296 — 57343.

Characters are displayed as patterns of dots. Each character position on the screen is composed of an 8 × 8 square of dots (pixels). Character memory contains the information which tells the computer which dots to turn on or off for a particular character. If a bit is 1, the dot is on (displayed in character colour). If it is 0, the dot is off (displayed in background colour). Therefore, to cover 64 dots, each character representation takes 8 bytes of memory.

e.g. The character 'A'

	128 64 32 16 8 4 2 1	Binary	Decimal Equivalent
byte 0		0 0 0 1 1 0 0 0	24
1		0 0 1 0 0 1 0 0	36
2		0 1 0 0 0 0 1 0	66
3		0 1 1 1 1 1 1 0	126
4		0 1 0 0 0 0 1 0	66
5		0 1 0 0 0 0 1 0	66
6		0 1 0 0 0 0 1 0	66
7		0 0 0 0 0 0 0 0	0

As mentioned earlier, the screen codes act as pointers into character memory. As you can see from the table in Appendix A the screen code for A in character set 1 is 1. Its 8 byte representation is therefore stored in:

53248 + (8*1) = 53256 and the next 7 bytes

so byte 53256 contains the value 24
so byte 53257 contains the value 36
so byte 53258 contains the value 66
so byte 53259 contains the value 126
so byte 53260 contains the value 66
so byte 53261 contains the value 66
so byte 53262 contains the value 66
so byte 53263 contains the value 00

In general, to find the starting address of the representation of a character with screen code X use:

53248 + (8*X)   for character set 1
55296 + (8*X)   for character set 2

You can change from one character set to the other from the keyboard as described earlier, or by changing the value of the character memory pointer — byte 53272. Its value is normally 21 (upper case and graphics) or 23 (upper and lower case).

Designing your own characters

Since the built-in character sets are in ROM you cannot directly change them. However, as you have seen, the character memory pointer can be changed. So the secret to using a character set you design yourself is to change the pointer to point to your set.

First, however, you must design your characters. Take a piece of graph paper (or draw an 8 × 8 grid), and for each special character you want, set it up as below. As an example, our grid contains a hat character.

	128	64	32	16	8	4	2	1	Binary	Decimal
byte 0									0 0 1 1 1 1 0 0	60
1									0 0 1 1 1 1 0 0	60
2									0 0 1 1 1 1 0 0	60
3									0 0 1 1 1 1 0 0	60
4									0 0 1 1 1 1 0 0	60
5									0 0 1 1 1 1 0 0	60
6									1 1 1 1 1 1 1 1	255
7									0 0 0 0 0 0 0 0	0

Fill in the squares to create the character you want. Then, for each row, add up the values of the squares filled in. The sum is the value you will POKE into the byte.

It is usual to copy some of the built in character set into RAM and then change those characters you wish to.

A sample exercise should clarify this.

Type POKE 53272, 28

All characters on the screen should now turn to random dots, since the character memory pointer now points to an area of memory where no characters have been defined — the bytes here contain random values. STOP   RESTORE will return you to the normal character memory.

Now run the following program:

```
5   REM * CHARACTER GENERATION DEMO *
10  POKE 53272, 28
20  POKE 52, 48 : POKE 56, 48 : CLR
30  POKE 56334, PEEK (56334) AND 254
40  POKE 1, PEEK (1) AND 251
50  FOR J = 0 TO 511
60  POKE 12288 + J, PEEK (53248 + J)
70  NEXT
80  POKE 1, PEEK (1) OR 4
90  POKE 56334, PEEK (56334) OR 1
100 PRINT "A"
110 FOR J = 12296 TO 12303 : READ V : POKE J, V: NEXT
120 DATA 60, 60, 60, 60, 60, 60, 255, 0
```

Explanation:

Line   10— changes the character memory pointer — character
                 memory now starts at 7168
             20— makes sure that BASIC doesn't overwrite the
                 character set

84

30— turn off interrupts

40— switch character ROM in

50-70— copies the first 64 characters (512 bytes) from character set 1 in ROM to RAM, starting at 7168

80— switch out character ROM

90— turn on interrupts

100— prints an 'A'

110— changes the definition of 'A' in character memory to a hat

120— Data statement holding the values of the new definition of 'A'

Note that all A's displayed on the screen change.

Where to put the new character set

A safe (but not the only) place to put character memory is at 12288. To do this POKE 53272, 28.

To ensure that BASIC doesn't overwrite your character set you must change the pointers to the end of BASIC program memory and the end of string storage memory. If you are starting character memory at 12288, you can protect it by using:

POKE 52, 48 : POKE 56, 48 : CLR

This should be done before any BASIC variables are defined or referenced, otherwise BASIC may not recognise the limitation.

Having done the above, you may now POKE in your new character set, starting at 12288. Remember that screen codes act as pointers into character memory, so if you POKE a value of 7 into screen memory, the eighth character in the set will be displayed.

For those who wish to put character memory elsewhere, or use a larger set, the following details will be useful.

In fact, both screen and character memory pointers can be changed. Byte 53272 controls both. The first 4 bits gives the number of K (1024) bytes from 0 to the start of screen memory. The last 4 bits gives the number of K bytes from 0 to the start of character memory.

However, to complicate matters, both of these numbers are calculated using addresses as seen by the Video Interface Chip. It uses different addresses to the rest of the computer to access the same locations. The table below illustrates the differing addresses for the memory blocks the VIC chip can access.

VIC chip addresses	Ordinary addresses	Memory
4096	53248	Upper case characters
4608	53760	Graphics characters
5120	54272	Reversed upper case
5632	54784	Reversed graphics
6144	55296	Lower case
6656	55808	Upper case and graphics
7168	56320	Reversed lower case
7680	56832	Reversed upper case & graphics

Example calculation of value of byte 53272. To put screen memory at 1024, character memory at 12888:

Address	No. of K from 0
Screen - 1024	$1024/1024 = 1$
Character - 12288	$12288/1024 = 12$

Binary representation of byte 53272	Screen mem 0001	Char mem 1100	$= 28$

To calculate it in decimal, use:

    (16 * Screen memory pointer) + Character memory pointer

        $(16 * 1) + 12 = 28$

So, POKE 53272, 28

To calculate the POKE values of bytes 52 and 56, work out the number of ¼K bytes (256) from 0 to the start of character memory. Use ordinary addresses, not the VIC chip addresses.

In this example it is $12288/256 = 48$

so POKE 52, 48 : POKE 56, 48 : CLR

Bytes 55, 56 indicate the end of BASIC program memory.

Bytes 51, 52 indicate the start of BASIC string storage.

Bytes 51 and 55 are 0 after a CLR or RUN and so can be ignored.

Some programs, such as the Programmer's Aide, check byte 644 instead of 55, 56 to find the end of BASIC memory. To avoid these overwriting your character set you should POKE the same value into 644, if you're using such a program.

High Resolution Graphics

In low resolution graphics, characters are the focus of attention. You define characters, you move characters around and so on. In high resolution graphics the dots (pixels) which make up the characters are the focus of attention. The difference between the two is in programming technique, not in the way in which things are displayed.

Typically, in low resolution, the character set, once defined, is not changed, while the screen memory is. In high resolution, screen memory, once defined, is not changed, while character memory is. The trick is to think of character memory not as defining characters, but as defining the screen - one bit in character memory controlling one pixel on the screen.

The following program demonstrates high-resolution plotting:

First, we set up our high-res screen and clear it

```
5 REM * HIRES PLOTTING *
10 POKE53272,29          :REM MOVE SCREEN
20 POKE53265,59          :REM HIRES BIT MODE
30 FORJ=8192TO16191
40 POKEJ,0
50 NEXT
```

Next we POKE in the background colour by POKEing the colour codes into Screen memory

```
60 FORJ=1024TO2023
70 POKE J,16
80 NEXT
90 :
```

Finally a small routine to enable control of pixel plotting by using the A, D, W and X keys

```
100 POKE 650,128
110 HR=8192
120 GET A$: IF A$=""THEN120
130 IFA$="A"THENX=X-1
140 IFA$="D"THENX=X+1
150 IFA$="W"THENY=Y-1
160 IFA$="X"THENY=Y+1
```

The following lines calculate the next pixel position and perform a boundary test before plotting the next point

```
200 P=HR+INT(Y/8)*320+8*INT(X/8)+(YAND7)
210 IFP<8192ORP>16191THEN120
220 POKE P,PEEK(P)OR(2↑(7-(XAND7)))
230 GOTO 120
```

This creates a 320 x 200 pixel hi resolution screen. Now, to change a pixel, we merely need to change the bit in character memory corresponding to it. If we consider the high resolution work area as a 320 × 200 grid:

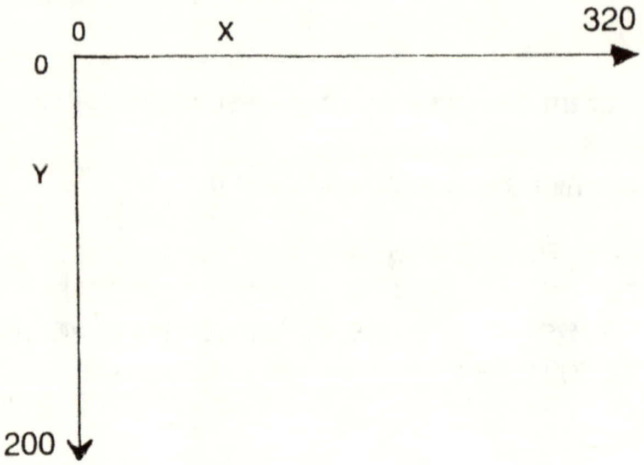

we can give any pixel X and Y co-ordinates and work out the bit to change as follows:

```
CHAR = INT (X/8)
ROW = INT (Y/8)
BYTE = 8192 + ROW * 320 + CHAR * 8 + (Y AND 7)
BIT = 7 - (X AND 7)
```

To turn 1 bit on while leaving the other bits in the byte unchanged, OR a mask with the current value of the byte.

e.g. POKE BYTE, PEEK (BYTE) OR (2 ↑ BIT)

Suppose we want to turn on the pixel with co-ordinates (35, 32). For the sake of the example assume the relevant byte has a value of 47. Using the formulae above we get:

POKE 9504, PEEK (9504) OR 2 ↑ 4

2 ↑ 4	0 0 0 1 0 0 0 0
OR PEEK (9504)	0 0 1 0 1 1 1 1
gives	0 0 1 1 1 1 1 1

To turn off a bit, AND NOT a mask with the current value of the byte

e.g. POKE BYTE, PEEK (BYTE) AND NOT (2 ↑ BIT)

To turn off the bit we just turned on

POKE 9504, PEEK (9504) AND NOT (2 ↑ 4)

2 ↑ 4	0 0 0 1 0 0 0 0
NOT 2 ↑ 4	1 1 1 0 1 1 1 1
AND PEEK (9504)	0 0 1 1 1 1 1 1
gives	0 0 1 0 1 1 1 1

The following example program plots a sine curve on the high resolution area.

```
10 REM * SINE WAVE *
20 FORJ=8192TO16191 :POKEJ,0:NEXT
30 POKE53272,29:POKE53265,59
40 POKE53280,0:POKE53281,0
50 PRINT CHR$(147)
60 FOR J=1024TO2023:POKEJ,16:NEXT
100 FORX=0TO320
110 Y=100+SIN(X/50)*100:GOSUB200
120 NEXTX
130 GOTO130
200 LINE=YAND7
210 BYTE=8192+INT(Y/8)*320+INT(X/8)*8+LINE
220 BIT=7-(XAND7)
230 POKEBYTE,PEEK(BYTE)OR(2↑BIT)
240 RETURN
```

Unfortunately, BASIC is too slow for most high resolution applications. It is generally better to use machine language programs which are many times faster.

Multicolour Characters

So far, each character position has been restricted to 2 colours - background and character. At the expense of resolution, it is possible to add two more colours - border and auxiliary.

Instead of a character position being 8 × 8 dots, in multicolour mode it is 4 × 8 dots - i.e. it takes 2 bits to define a dot, which is now 2 pixels wide. e.g.

screen dot	3	2	1	0
character byte	1 0	0 0	0 1	1 1

The colours selected by each 2 bits are as follows:

Bit Pair	COLOUR REGISTER	LOCATION
0 0	Background #0 (screen colour)	53281
0 1	Background #1	53282
1 0	Background #2	53283
1 1	Lower 3 bits in colour memory	Colour RAM

When designing multi-coloured characters, the POKE values for character memory are calculated exactly as for normal characters.

You know how to set background, border and character colours. The auxiliary colour can be any of the 16 background colours - the following codes apply:

0 - Black	8 - Orange
1 - White	9 - Brown
2 - Red	10 - Light Red
3 - Cyan	11 - Grey — 1
4 - Purple	12 - Grey — 2
5 - Green	13 - Light Green
6 - Blue	14 - Light Blue
7 - Yellow	15 - Grey — 3

It is set by POKEing the relevant value into the locations from the bit-pair table.

The video chip must be made to interpret character memory bytes as multicoloured. To do this, bit 4 of location 53270 must be set to 1 and bit 3 of each colour memory byte that you want multicoloured must be set to 1. So when you POKE the colour codes into colour memory add 8 to the normal codes. The same technique applies to characters PRINTed. POKEing the usual code + 8 into byte 646 will make the Video chip interpret character codes as multicoloured characters when PRINTing.

Multicolour and normal resolution characters may be mixed by setting the 4th bit on some colour memory nybbles and not on others.

EXTENDED BACKGROUND COLOUR MODE

The single additional ability given to you in this mode is the ability to control the background colour of a character position on the screen independent of the global background colour.

However, once this mode is selected, you can only address the first 64 characters in your programmable character set. This is because two of the bits of the character code are used to select the background colour. Use the following table to select the extended background colours for characters POKEd onto the screen.

Character range	Background Colour Register
0 — 63	53281
64 — 127	53282
128 — 191	53283
192 — 255	53284

To select extended background colour mode, use:
POKE 53265, PEEK(53265) OR 64

MULTICOLOUR BIT MAP MODE

Multicolour bit map mode works in the same way as standard bit map mode except that plotting is done in multicolour. This mode suffers the same resolution loss as multicolour mode owing to the bit pair colour representation. The bit pairs don't represent the same colour information as in multicolour mode. The bit pair colour table for multicolour bit map mode is as follows:

Bits	Colour information
0 0	Background colour #0
0 1	Upper 4 bits of screen memory
1 0	Lower 4 bits of screen memory
1 1	Lower 4 bits of colour memory for that byte

Multicolour bit map mode is selected by setting bit 5 in location 53265 and bit 4 of location 53270.

Use the following BASIC statement to achieve this:

POKE 53265, PEEK(53265) OR 32 : POKE 53270, PEEK(53270) OR 16

SPRITES

A sprite is a form of user defined character that is controlled by a powerful video chip called the 6566. Up to 8 sprites can be displayed at a time automatically. More sprites can be displayed using Raster Interrupt techniques. Sprites have the following advantages over user defined characters:

1. Pixel by pixel movement in any direction
2. The 24 by 21 pixel sprite shape can be moved as though it were a single character
3. Magnification (2X) in both horizontal and vertical directions
4. Independent high-res/multicolour mode
5. Selectable sprite to background overlay priority
6. Sprite to sprite collision detection
7. Sprite to background collision detection.

A sprite is larger than a character therefore more data is needed to define the shape of a sprite. A sprite is 24 pixels (3 bytes) wide and 21 pixels high which gives us a total of 3 x 21 = 63 bytes of data to define the shape of a single sprite. Even though a single sprite is made up of so much data, the video chip moves the sprite as if it were a single character.

Sprite Pointers

The 64 byte blocks of data that define the shape of each sprite can be placed in any 64 byte multiple of unused memory. In order to tell the video chip where in memory each sprite-shape block is located, eight sprite pointers are provided.

The shape of a sprite may be changed by adjusting the sprite pointer allocated to that sprite to point to a different block of sprite-shape data. Using this method a single sprite may be animated by quickly changing the sprite's pointer to switch through a series of shapes provided for that sprites's animation (e.g. an explosion). Switching the pointer rather than switching between sprites leaves the other sprites free for other uses.

The sprite pointers are the last 8 bytes of unused screen memory (2040 — 2047). If you move screen memory, the pointers will move with it (but not their contents). You must remember when setting up your sprite pointers that the pointer must point to the first byte within the sprite and that the value in the sprite pointer is the actual memory location of the sprite over 64. Therefore, the following formula applies:

Location = Sprite pointer * 64

Also if you are not using video bank #0 (default bank) then you must also add bank number * 16384 to the location. If you haven't switched video banks, then don't worry.

Two important points to remember when choosing where to put your sprite data in memory are 1, its location **must** be a multiple of 64, and 2, check the memory map to make sure that you are only using spare memory.

Turning Sprites On

For a sprite to be displayed to the screen, it must be turned on. The memory location where the video chip gets its information on which sprites should be turned on and which should be turned off is location 53269. The 8 bits within byte 53269 are labled from right to left 0 — 7. Therefore, if we label our sprites from 0 — 7 then we easily determine which sprites should be on and which should be off by the value contained in byte 53269. The way that the on/off status of each sprite is determined is a follows:

A 1 in the bit corresponding to the sprite determines that the sprite should be displayed (turned on) and a 0 determines that the sprite should not be displayed (turned off).

e.g.   7 6 5 4 3 2 1 0
        1 1 0 1 0 1 1 1 = 215

therefore the statement POKE 53269, 215 would supply the video chip with the following information:

Sprites 7, 6, 4, 2, 1 and 0 are to be turned on.

Sprites 5 and 3 are to be turned off.

To turn on a single sprite without effecting the others, use the following statement:

POKE 53269, PEEK (53269) OR (2 ↑ SN)

where SN is the sprite number (0 — 7)

To turn off a single sprite without effecting the others, use the following statement:

POKE 53269, PEEK (53269) AND (255 − 2 ↑ SN)

Sprite colour

High resolution (single colour) sprites can be any one of the 16 colours. The colour of each sprite 0 — 7 should be POKEd into their respective colour registers, memory locations 53287 — 53294 (see video register map). Each pixel turned on within the sprite will be displayed in the colour determined by the sprite's colour register. Each pixel turned off will be displayed in the colour behind the sprite (i.e. it is transparent).

Multicolour Sprites

In multicolour mode, it is possible to have four different colours in each sprite. Though, as with multicoloured characters, multicoloured sprites have only half the resolution of single coloured sprite (ie. pixels must be displayed in pairs). The following table gives the colours determined by each bit-pair combination.

Bit pair	Resultant Colour
00	Transparent (screen colour)
01	Sprite multicolour register #0 (location 53285)
10	Sprite-colour register
11	Sprite multicolour register #1 (location 53286)

The register that holds information on which sprites are multicolored and which sprites are not is mapped to location 53276.
To set a sprite to multicolour, use the following statement:
POKE 53276, PEEK(53276) OR (2 ↑ SN)
where SN is the sprite number (0 — 7).
To switch a sprite out of multicolour mode, us the following statement.
POKE 53276, PEEK (53276) AND (255 − 2 ↑ SN)

Expanding Sprites

Sprites can be expanded vertically, horizontally or both. A sprite is expanded by putting 2 pixels in place of 1 and 2 blanks in place of 1 in the direction of expansion thus giving a 2X expansion. To expand a sprite horizontally, the corresponding bit in location 53277 must be set to 1. To unexpand the sprite, the bit must be set to 0. Vertical expansion is done in the same way using location 53271. The POKE statements to control expansion and unexpansion of sprites are as follows:
Horizontal expansion
POKE 53277, PEEK (53277) OR (2 ↑ SN)
Horizontal unexpansion
POKE 53277, PEEK (53277) AND (255 − 2 ↑ SN)
Vertical expansion
POKE 53271, PEEK (53271) OR (2 ↑ SN)
Vertical unexpansion
POKE 53271, PEEK (53271) AND (255 − 2 ↑ SN)
where SN is the sprite number from 0 — 7.

Sprite Movement

Sprites are moved around the display by changing the values in each sprites's horizontal and vertical position registers. These registers are mapped to memory location 53248 to 53263 and a most-significant-bit (MSB) register at location 53264. The MSB register is used to rectify the problem of horizontal screen width. The MSB register works as follows. In order to gain pixel by pixel movement, the horizontal position register needs to be able to hold values from 0 to 299 (screen width). A single register can only hold values from 0 to 255 therefore we need at least one more bit to handle values up to 299. An extra bit (9th bit) would allow us control over positions 0 to 511. This is the purpose of the MSB register. The bits in the MSB register correspond to the sprite number. (ie. bit 0 for sprite 0, bit 1 for sprite 1, etc.) A register map of all sprite positioning registers is as follows:

Location	Use of Register
53248	Sprite 0 X position
53249	Sprite 0 Y position
53250	Sprite 1 X position
53251	Sprite 1 Y position
53252	Sprite 2 X position
53253	Sprite 2 Y position
53254	Sprite 3 X position
53255	Sprite 3 Y position
53256	Sprite 4 X position
53257	Sprite 4 Y position
53258	Sprite 5 X position
53259	Sprite 5 Y position
53260	Sprite 6 X position
53261	Sprite 6 Y position
53262	Sprite 7 X position
53263	Sprite 7 Y position
53264	Sprite (0 — 7) MSB register

Note that horizontal positions 24 and 344 are the left and right boundaries of the screen. Sprites continue to move outside this range but cannot be seen.

It's about time we had a look at one of these sprites. Study the following program and its comments. Type it in and run it.

```
1 REM *** SQUARE ***
5 REM   *CLEAR THE SCREEN TO BLUE WITH A BLACK
BORDER
```

```
10 PRINTCHR$(147):POKE53230,0:POKE53281,6
15 REM  *SET SPRITE-POINTER #0 TO POINT TO
LOCATION 13*64=832
20 POKE 2040,13
25 REM  *CREATE A SQUARE SPRITE IN MEMORY
LOCATIONS 832 TO 832+63
30 FOR MEM=832 TO 834:POKE MEM,255:NEXT
40 FOR MEM=835 TO 839 STEP 3
50 POKE MEM,128:POKEMEM+1,0:POKEMEM+2,1
60 NEXT MEM
70 FORMEM=892TO894:POKEMEM,255:NEXT
75 REM  *SET BEGINNING OF VIDEO CHIP
80 VIDEO=53248
85 REM  *TURN ON SPRITE #0
90 POKE VIDEO+21,1
95 REM  *CHOOSE THE COLOUR WHITE FOR SPRITE #0
100 POKE VIDEO+39,1
109 REM *MOVE SPRITE ACROSS SCREEN
110 Y=100 : POKE VIDEO+1,Y:FOR X=0 TO 347
115 REM *CALCULATE X-POSITION AND MSB
120 MSB=INT(X/256) : XP=X-256*MSB
130 POKE VIDEO+0,XP: POKE VIDEO+16,MSB
140 NEXT X
```

Run the program and you should see a square sprite float across the screen.
• To expand the sprite in the horizontal and vertical directions before moving, add the following line:
105 POKE VIDEO + 29, 1 : POKE VIDEO + 23, 1
and run the program again.
The following program allows you to use the cursor keys to draw a sprite by editing DATA statements. Type RUN 1, then use the cursor keys to move around the DATA statements. Use the shift Q character to signify a pixel-ON and a full-stop to signify a pixel-OFF. When you have finished drawing your sprite, move the cursor to the top of the screen, then keep hitting the RETURN key until you have entered all of the DATA statements. Now type RUN, and the program will generate the sprites and the DATA statements needed to generate that sprite. To store these DATA statements, use the same method as you used on the last set of DATA statements.

```
0 GOTO10
1 PRINTCHR$(147):POKE53269,0:LIST29-50
10 PRINTCHR$(147):FORI=0TO63:POKE832+I,0:NEXT
```

```
15 POKE53280,6:POKE53281,6
20 GOTO 60
29 REM...01234567890123456789 0123
30 DATA "•..••••••••••••••••••••••"
31 DATA "••..•••••••••••••••••••••"
32 DATA "•.•..•••••••••••••••••••"
33 DATA "•..•..•••••••••••••••••"
34 DATA "•...•..•••••••••••••••"
35 DATA "•....•..•••••••••••••"
36 DATA "•.....•..•••••••••••"
37 DATA "•......•..•••••••••••"
38 DATA "•.......•..••••••••••"
39 DATA "•........•..••••••••"
40 DATA "•.........•..•••••••"
41 DATA "•..........•..•••••••"
42 DATA "•...........•..••••••"
43 DATA "•............•..•••••"
44 DATA "•.............•..••••"
45 DATA "•..............•..•••"
46 DATA "•...............•..•••"
47 DATA "•................•..••"
48 DATA "•.................•..••"
49 DATA "•..................•..••"
50 DATA "••••••••••••••••••••..•"
60 V=53248:POKEV+16,1:POKEV+1,50 :POKEV+21,
   1:POKEV+39,3:POKE2040,13
70 POKEV+23,1:POKEV+29,1
80 FORI=0TO20:PRINT1000+I;"DATA";:READA$:FORK=
   0TO2:T=0:FORJ=0TO7:B=0
90 IF MID$(A$,J+K*8+1,1)="•"THENB=1
100 T=T+B*2↑(7-J):NEXT:PRINT T;",";:POKE 832+
   I*3+K,T:NEXT:PRINT"▮ ":NEXT
110 END
3000 PRINTCHR$(19):END
9000 SAVE"@0:SPRITE",8
9010 VERIFY"SPRITE",8
```

SPRITE DISPLAY PRIORITIES

Sprite priority determines if the sprite should appear in front or behind
another background. If the background is another sprite, then the priority
is fixed by the sprite's sprite number. Sprite 0 has the highest priority,
sprite 1 has the next priority, and so on, up to sprite 7. For example, if

sprite 0 and sprite 7 are positioned so that they cross each other, sprite 0 will be in front of sprite 7, though you would be able to see sprite 7 through sprite 0 (unless of course sprite 0 was a completely filled square). Sprite to background priority is more flexible in the way that each sprite can be set with priority above or below the background. The sprite to background priorities are controlled by the sprite priority register (memory location 53275). A 1 in the bit number corresponding to the sprite number will set that sprite with a lower priority than the background. A 0 in this bit position will give the sprite a higher priority than the background. By moving sprites back and forth over other objects, at the same time changing the sprite-background priorities, it is possible to make it look as if the sprites are moving in front and behind the object thus creating a three dimensional effect.

The following program overlays 8 sprites to demonstrate sprite priority:

```
5 REM * DEMONSTRATING EIGHT SPRITES *
10 POKE53280,6:POKE53281,0
20 PRINT CHR$(147);"CREATING SPRITES"
30 POKE 52,62 :POKE 56,62 :P=248
40 FOR MEM=2040TO2047:POKEMEM,P:P=P+1
50 NEXT MEM
51 :
60 BYTE=272
70 FOR SN=0 TO 7 : PRINT SN
80 LOC=PEEK(2040+SN)*64
90 BYTE=BYTE/2:B=BYTE:ROW=0
100 FORMEM=LOCTOLOC+63STEP3
110  IFSN =3THEN140
120 ROW=ROW+1:T=(ROW-SN-3)/4:B=0
130 IF INT(T)=T THEN B=255
140 FOR COL=0TO2:POKEMEM+COL,B:NEXT COL
150 NEXT MEM,SN
155 :
160 VIDEO=53248:A=150:B=0
170 POKE VIDEO+21,255:POKE VIDEO+28,255
175 POKE VIDEO+37,1:POKE VIDEO+38,1
180 C=0:FOR R=39 TO 46:C=1
190 POKE VIDEO+R,C:PRINTCHR$(147):NEXTR
200 I=A:A=B:B=I:D=SGN(B-A)
210 FOR SN=7 TO 0 STEP-1
215 Z=11*(SN>3)*(A=0)
220 PRINT CHR$(147);"SPRITE";SN
```

```
230 SX=VIDEO+SN*2:SY=SX+1
240 Y=A-D+Z:FORX=A+ZTOB+ZSTEPD:Y=Y+D
250 POKE SX,X:POKE SY,Y
260 NEXT X,SN
270 FOR PAUSE=1TO2000:NEXT
290 GOTO 200
```

Sprite Collisions

Sprite collisions are detected by the computer and collision information is stored in location 53278 for sprite to sprite collisions and location 53279 for sprite to another background collision. The bit set to 1 in each of these registers corresponds to the sprite involved in the collision. The bit stays set until the register is read (PEEKed). So if the collision information is to be used more than once per collision, it would be a good idea to store the value into a variable. Also, programs that use the sprite collision registers should include in their initialization a PEEK of each of these registers to clear them of previous collision data.

Note: A bit pair 01 in a multicoloured mode will not be detected in a sprite to background collision, even though it can be seen on the screen. So, for example, if you wish to have objects that should not cause a collision (e.g. a cloud) then they should be coloured by using bit pair 01 (multicolour register #01).

SELECTING A VIDEO BANK

Even though there is 64K of RAM (Random Access Memory) available, the video chip can only access 16K at any one time. The 16K block of RAM that your program will use depends on your particular application. The reason for this is that each of the 16K blocks have different memory allocations to character generation. Then there is the problem of BASIC residency. The following memory block descriptions should make this clear.

Memory Block	RAM seen by Video Chip	Character Set Used	Memory Usage
0	0—4095 and 8192—16383	ROM 4096—8191 (Standard)	System variables and default screen memory
1	16384—32767	RAM any 2K multiple (User generated)	Basic programs and variables (2048— 40959)
2	32768—36863 and 40960—49151	ROM 36864—40959 (Standard)	String space
3	49152—65535	RAM any 2K multiple (User generated)	

Two more things to remember when choosing a memory block are:-
• Sprites take up 64 bytes and their position in memory must be a 64 byte multiple.
• The high-res screen takes up 8K and its position in memory must be an 8K multiple.

As seen from the previous table, the more memory your BASIC program takes, the further up memory you will have to put your sprite data, hires screen and alternate character set if any of these are used; otherwise use the default screen at location 1024 — 2047.
The bank select bits that are used to select which of the four banks of 16K memory you wish the video chip to get all of its sprite data, character set and screen information from are bits 0 and 1 of location 53576. However, before changing the contents of this location to choose your video bank, you must first set bits 0 and 1 of location 56578 to 1. The BASIC statement to do this is as follows:
POKE 56578, PEEK (56578) OR 3
The BASIC statement to select the video bank is as follows:
POKE 56576, (PEEK (56576) AND 252) OR (3 − BANK)
where the value of BANK depends on the following table:

Value of BANK	BITS	BANK	STARTING LOCATION	VIC -II CHIP RANGE
0	00	0	0	0 — 16383 (Default bank)
1	01	1	16384	16384 — 32767
2	10	2	32768	32768 — 49151
3	11	3	41952	49152 — 65535

VIC-II CHIP REGISTER MAP

Reg. #	7	6	5	4	3	2	1	0	
0	Sprite# 0				x — position				
1	Sprite# 0				y — position				
2	Sprite# 1				x — position				
3	Sprite# 1				y — position				
4	Sprite# 2				x — position				
5	Sprite# 2				y — position				
6	Sprite# 3				x — position				
7	Sprite# 3				y — position				
8	Sprite# 4				x — position				
9	Sprite# 4				y — position				
10	Sprite# 5				x — position				
11	Sprite# 5				y — position				
12	Sprite# 6				x — position				
13	Sprite# 6				y — position				
14	Sprite# 7				x — position				
15	Sprite# 7				y — position				
16	Sprite #7	Sprite #6	Sprite #5	Sprite #4	Sprite #3	Sprite #2	Sprite #1	Sprite #0	MSB of x — position
17	—	EXTENDED Colour	Bit map	Display enable	Screen height	—	Vertical Scroll	—	Mode y - scroll
18	Raster register								
19	Light pen — x								
20	Light pen — y								
21	Sprite #7	Sprite #6	Sprite #5	Sprite #4	Sprite #3	Sprite #2	Sprite #1	Sprite #0	Sprite enable
22	—	—	Reset Multi	Multi colour	Screen width	—	Horizontal scroll	—	Multi colour x scroll
23	Sprite #7	Sprite #6	Sprite #5	Sprite #4	Sprite #3	Sprite #2	Sprite #1	Sprite #0	Sprite y — expand
24	Screen location				Character base			—	
25	IRQ	—	—	—	Light pen	Sprite-Sprite collision	Sprite-bgnd collision	Raster	Interrupt register
26	IRQ	—	—	—	Light pen	Sprite-Sprite collision	Sprite bgnd collision	Raster	Interupt enable
27	Sprite #7	Sprite #6	Sprite #5	Sprite #4	Sprite #3	Sprite #2	Sprite #1	Sprite #0	Sprite — background priority
28	Sprite #7	Sprite #6	Sprite #5	Sprite #4	Sprite #3	Sprite #2	Sprite #1	Sprite #0	Sprite multicolour select
29	Sprite #7	Sprite #6	Sprite #5	Sprite #4	Sprite #3	Sprite #2	Sprite #1	Sprite #0	Sprite x — expand
30	Sprite #7	Sprite #6	Sprite #5	Sprite #4	Sprite #3	Sprite #2	Sprite #1	Sprite #0	Sprite to Sprite collision
31	Sprite #7	Sprite #6	Sprite #5	Sprite #4	Sprite #3	Sprite #2	Sprite #1	Sprite #0	Sprite to background collision
32	Screen border Colour								
33	Background Colour #0								
34	Background Colour #1								
35	Background Colour #2								
36	Background Colour #3								
37	Sprite multicolour #0								
38	Sprite multicolour #1								
39	Sprite #0 Colour								
40	Sprite #1 Colour								
41	Sprite #2 Colour								
42	Sprite #3 Colour								
43	Sprite #4 Colour								
44	Sprite #5 Colour								
45	Sprite #6 Colour								
46	Sprite #7 Colour								

CHAPTER 6

MACHINE LANGUAGE PROGRAMMING ON THE COMMODORE 64

In this chapter, the following topics will be covered:

MICROPROCESSOR & MACHINE LANGUAGE
— Binary & Hexadecimal Numbering System
— Registers & Addressing
— Machine Code & Instruction Mnemonics
— Simple Machine Language Programs

MACHINE LANGUAGE PROGRAMMING ON COMMODORE 64
— Program Entry
— Program Execution
— Some Commodore 64 Useful Routines

MEMORY MAP & MANAGEMENT
— Memory Map & 'Shadow Zone'
— Memory Management
— Some Memory Configurations

COMMODORE 64 KERNAL
— Concepts of Kernal & Operating System
— Power-up Instructions
— Using Kernal Routines
— Simple Programs that Call Kernal Routines

MICROPROCESSOR & MACHINE LANGUAGE

INTRODUCTION

A microprocessor is the central processing and control unit of a microcomputer system just like the brain of a human being. As with any other electronic devices, the only way to communicate with a microprocessor chip is via electronic signal pulses. There are certain combinations of pulses that the microprocessor can understand which form the basis of a Machine Language. A group of all the 'words' that a microprocessor understands is called its instruction set.

Different microprocessors speak different machine languages. In a Commodore 64, the central microprocessor unit is named 6510. For those of you who have heard of the famous 6502 which can be found inside Apple, Atari and other Commodore models, 6510 is its cousin. It has the same instruction set as its better known relative. The only major difference is that 6510 has an inherent I/O port which makes it impossible to use the first two bytes of RAM.

BINARY & HEXADECIMAL NUMBERING SYSTEM

In the eyes of a microprocessor, an electronic signal can only have either one of the two states — a '0' or a '1'. As we are going to work with a microprocessor, we had better learn its numbering system, called binary, in which every number is made up of a bunch of '0' bits or '1' bits (BIT is an acronym for BInary digiT). The 6510 processor is an 8-bit machine which means all the numbers it knows range from 00000000, 00000001, 00000010, ... up to 11111111.

For those of you mathematicians, the largest number is:

$$1 \times 2^7 + 1 \times 2^6 + 1 \times 2^5 + 1 \times 2^4 + 1 \times 2^3 + 1 \times 2^2 + 1 \times 2^1 + 1 \times 2^0 = 255$$

in our human decimal system. The conversion between binary and decimal numbers is by no means a trivial exercise. (Can you tell immediately whether 10111010 is larger than 180?) An intermediate numbering system was invented to facilitate conversion to and from binary numbers and on the other hand save the finger-counting feats. It is called hexadecimal which means 1 digit has 16 counts. Conversion with binary numbers is simple because this one digit can represent all combinations of 4 bits.

Conversion Table of Hexadecimal, Binary and Decimal
Note: 6502 programmers' % $ convention of prefixing binary and hexadecimal numbers. Decimal numbers do not have a prefix.

Decimal Count	Binary Bits	Hexadecimal Digit
0	%0000	$0
1	0001	1
2	0010	2
3	0011	3
4	0100	4
5	0101	5
6	0110	6
7	0111	7
8	1000	8
9	1001	9
10	1010	A
11	1011	B
12	1100	C
13	1101	D
14	1110	E
15	1111	F

1. HEXADECIMAL — BINARY CONVERSION

It is a straight-forward table look-up exercise once you remember 1 hexadecimal digit is equivalent to 4 bits. Always start conversion from the least significant digit (ie. rightmost digit).

Example:

$$\% \quad \underset{\$\ \ 2}{10}\ \underset{D}{1101}\ \underset{7}{0111}\ \underset{8}{1000}$$

2. HEXADECIMAL — DECIMAL CONVERSION

Conversion with decimals requires more arithmetic

a) Hexadecimal to Decimal

Look-up the decimal equivalent of each hex. digit before multiplying it by its 'weight' factor.

Example:

$$\$\quad 2 \qquad D \qquad 7 \qquad 8$$
$$2 \times 16^3 + 13 \times 16^2 + 7 \times 16 + 8 = 11640$$

It might be slightly simpler to work from the most significant digit (ie. leftmost digit) in this case:-

(i) multiply the digit by 16
(ii) add the digit to its right
(iii) iterate from (i) unless it is the last digit.

Example:

$$\$\quad 2 \qquad D \qquad 7 \qquad 8$$
$$(\,(2 \times 16 + 13) \times 16 + 7) \times 16 + 8 = 11640$$

b) Decimal to Hexadecimal

Divide the decimal number by 16 repeatedly. Convert remainders to hex representation.

Example:

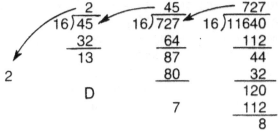

$$11640 \rightarrow \$2D78$$

3. DECIMAL — BINARY CONVERSION

This is best done by converting the original number to its hexadecimal equivalent and complete the conversion to the desired number system.

REGISTERS & ADDRESSING MODES

A. 6510 PROCESSOR REGISTERS

Registers are the actual working vehicles inside a microprocessor. They hold the crucial data for processing. All 6510 registers except one are 8-bits wide. The exception is the Program Counter which is 16-bits wide enabling the processor to address 2^{16} or 64K bytes of memory.

1. ACCUMULATOR (A)

The Accumulator is responsible for data manipulations such as memory load/store, addition/subtraction and other logical operations. Hence, it is often regarded as the most important register. In fact, if there ever exists a microprocessor with 2 registers only, one of them must be the accumulator.

2. X and Y INDEX REGISTERS (X, Y)

The primary function of an index register is to point at a memory location for data manipulations. Other uses of an index register include temporary storage, counter and memory load/store.

The 6510 has 2 index registers which makes indexing very efficient. They differ slightly from each other in the most advanced addressing modes. X index register specialises in Index Indirect addressing while Y index register is for Indirect Index addressing. This will be explained in detail when we talk about Addressing Modes later on.

3. STACK POINTER (SP)

A stack is a very important data structure in microprocessor programming or in fact in any computer. It is a block of memory where temporary storage is available. Data are stored on a Last-In, First-Out (LIFO)basis. You can imagine it as a stack of plates, where the one on top is the one most recently added and will be the first one to be removed.

The Stack Pointer is an 8-bit register that keeps track of the next available location or the top of the stack. In 6510, the stack is assigned to page 1 of memory (ie. address $0100 — $01FF) so that the high order address is always $01. The stack pointer is initialized at $FF and decrements towards $00 when something is pushed onto the stack.

The stack is used by the processor intrinsically to store the return address when a subroutine is called or when an interrupt occurs. It can also be used by programs that require data storage/retrieval in a LIFO fashion.

4. PROCESSOR STATUS REGISTER (PS or SR)

The Process Status Register is 8-bits wide and consists of 7 flags which indicate various status of the processor.

```
bit 7                                    bit 0
| N | V |   | B | D | I | Z | C |
```

Processor Status Register Flags

a) Negative or Sign Flag (N)
— Set when the result byte of an operation has its bit 7 set (showing a negative number in 2's compliment representation)

b) Overflow Flag (V)
— Set when an operation results in a carry from bit 6 into bit 7 (showing an overflow in case of 2's compliment addition/subtraction)

c) Break Flag (B)
— Set when an interrupt is caused by a BRK instruction (not by a hardware interrupt)

d) Decimal Flag (D)
— Set to let the processor operate in decimal of BCD mode (not binary mode)

e) Interrupt Disable Flag (I)
— Set to disable any interrupt from hardware interrupt request.

f) Zero Flag (Z)
— Set when an operation results in a zero byte or equality in a comparison

g) Carry Flag (C)
— Set when an operation results in a carry/no-borrow in an addition/subtraction. It also serves as the 9th bit extension of the accumulator in a shift/rotate operation. It is sometimes used as a user flag because it is easily programmable and does not have any effect on most operations.

5. INPUT/OUTPUT PORT

This unique I/O port of 6510 actually has 2 registers. At address $0000 is a Data Direction Register which controls the direction of traffic of the individual I/O lines. At address $0001 is the Data Register or the port itself.

6. PROGRAM COUNTER (PC)

The Program Counter is the only 16-bit register in the processor. Its sole function is to keep track of where the program is heading. It always points at the memory location from where the processor fetches its next instruction. Remember the processor with only 2 registers? A program counter is the other crucial register besides an accumulator.

B. ADDRESSING MODES

Addressing modes are the various fashions in which the processor specifies or addresses an operand. In 6510, there are 9 addressing modes, some of which have several names:-

105

— implied, implicit or intrinsic addressing (including accumulator addressing)
— immediate addressing
— absolute, absolute direct or extended addressing
— zero-page or zero-page direct addressing
— relative addressing
— indirect addressing
— indexed addressing (including zero-page indexed addressing)
— indexed indirect or pre-indexed indirect addressing
— indirect indexed or post-indexed indirect addressing

1. IMPLIED ADDRESSING (INCLUDING ACCUMULATOR ADDRESSING)

Implied addressing is used by single-byte instructions to operate on registers. Operands need not be specified; they are implied by the instructions themselves. Instructions using this addressing mode include register-register transfers, status flags set/clear, stack push/pop, etc.
Example:
TAX — transfer accumulator to X index register
CLC — clear carry flag
RTS — return from subroutine (modifies SP and PC)

2. IMMEDIATE ADDRESSING

The operands, mostly 8-bit constants, follow the instruction opcodes immediately. Instructions that use this addressing mode include register loads, arithmetic/logical operations and comparisons.
Example:
LDX #255 — load X index register with 255 or $FF
AND #$80 — logical AND accumulator with bit 7 only
CPY #0 — compare Y index register with 0

3. ABSOLUTE ADDRESSING

With this addressing mode, the 2 bytes that follow an opcode specify the effective address of the operand. All instructions that work with an operand in memory can use this addressing mode.
Example:
ADC $1100 — add contents of memory location $1100 to accumulator
EOR $D004 — logical exclusive-OR accumulator with contents of location $D004
JSR $1234 — jump to subroutine at $1234

4. ZERO-PAGE ADDRESSING

This is similar to absolute addressing except that the operand lies in page 0 ($0000 — $00FF). The instruction will be 2 bytes long only because 1 byte is sufficient to specify any location in the page 0. Variables that are often manipulated by a program should be stored in page 0 to take advantage of the memory efficiency of this addressing mode. Instructions that use this addressing mode are similar to those which can use the absolute addresing except the 2 jump instructions — JMP and JSR which always require a 16-bit address.

Example:

STY $12 — store Y index register at $0012

INC $20 — increment memory location at $0020 (by 1)

5. RELATIVE ADDRESSING

Relative addressing is used exclusively by Test and Branch instructions which are 2 bytes long. The first byte is an opcode which tells what test to perform. The second byte is a signed offset or relative count which tells how many bytes to branch forwards or backwards if the test succeeds.

Example:

BNE −128 — branch backwards 128 bytes if Zero Flag is clear.

BMI +127 — branch forwards 127 bytes if Negative Flag is set

(Note: −128 and +127 are maximum branch limits)

BCC 0 — no effect ; always proceed with next instruction regardless of the test result.

6. INDIRECT ADDRESSING

This addressing mode is only used by 1 instruction in 6510 — JMP. With this addressing mode, the destination of the jump operation is secified by 2 consecutive memory locations whose address follows the JMP opcode. Such locations that store destinations are known as Vectors.

Example:

JMP ($0300) — jumps to location whose address is found in memory $0300 (low order) and $0301 (high order)

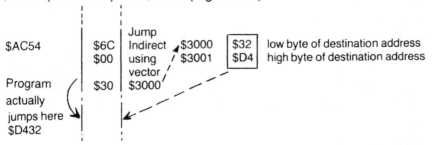

7. INDEXED ADDRESSING (INCLUDING ZERO-PAGE INDEXED ADDRESSING)

The effective address of the operand is determined by adding the contents of the index register (X or Y) to the base address. This base address can be 1 byte or 2 bytes long, depending on whether it is in page 0 or not. This addressing mode is useful when a range of memory locations (less than 256 bytes) is processed sequentially such as a block move.

Example:
LDA $10,X — load accumulator with contents of address $10 + X
STA $0310,Y — store accumulator at location Y bytes away from $0310

8. INDEXED INDIRECT ADDRESSING

This addressing mode only works with the X index register and a table of indirect pointers in page 0. The effective address of the operand is found in 2 consecutive memory locations whose address is the sum of the content of X index register and the base address in page 0. This addressing mode is useful when you have several possible operands which are pointed to by a table of indirect pointers and the X index register can decide which one in the table.

(Note: Remember that each entry of indirect pointers is 2-bytes long and hence the X index register should generally be a multiple of 2)
Example:
LDX #2
LDA ($40,X) — load accumulator with a memory byte whose address is specified in $42 (low order) and $43 (high order)

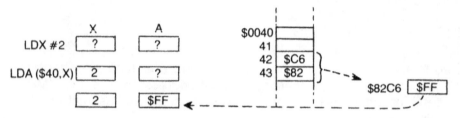

9. INDIRECT INDEXED ADDRESSING

This addressing mode only works with the Y index register and a table of data whose base address is stored as pointers in page 0. The effective address of the operand is the sum of the content of the Y index register and the base address pointer found in 2 consecutive memory locations in page 0. This addressing mode is useful when you have several tables to process and their base addresses are stored as page 0 indirect pointers. A block move can be done very efficiently using this addressing mode.
Example:
LDY #3
LDA ($10),Y — load accumulator with the 4th entry of a table whose base address is stored in $10 and $11 (low, high order)

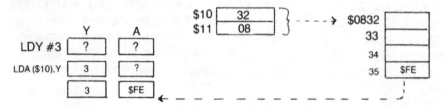

MACHINE CODE AND INSTRUCTION MNEMONICS

All the machine code instructions of an 8-bit microprocessor are made up of bytes. In 6510, the instructions are 1-byte, 2-bytes or 3-bytes long. To a microprocessor, all instructions are purely numbers but it will be extremely difficult for a human to write a program in a series of numbers. Mnemonic words are invented to help the programmers memorise each instruction.
For instance,

		A9
LDA #0		00
STA $D001	is more meaningful than	8D
		01
		D0

The 6510 instruction set can be classified into 4 groups by functions
— data transfer
— arithmetic and logical operations
— program control
— miscellaneous

MNEMONIC CONVENTIONS

Registers
A - Accumulator
X — X index register
Y — Y index register

P — Processor status register
S — Stack pointer

Processor Status Flags
C — Carry
D — Decimal

I — Interrupt disable
V — oVerflow

A. DATA TRANSFERS
1. Register — Register Transfer
   Format: Tpq — Transfer register p to register q
   Instructions: TAX, TXA, TAY, TYA, TXS, TSX
2. Register — Memory Transfers
   Format: LDp — LoaD register p with memory
   STq — STore register q into memory
   Instructions: LDA, LDX, LDY
   STA, STX, STY
3. Register — Stack Transfer
   Format: PHp — PusH register p onto the stack
   PLq — PulL register q off the stack
   Instructions: PHA, PHP
   PLA, PLP

B. ARITHMETIC AND LOGICAL OPERATIONS

1. Add/Subtract with Carry/Borrow
   Instructions: ADC, SBC
2. Increment/Decrement
   Instructions: INX, DEX, INY, DEY (index registers)
   INC, DEC (memory)
3. Logical AND, OR and Exclusive-OR
   Instructions: AND, ORA, EOR
4. Comparisons
   Instructions: CMP, CPX, CPY — comparisons with A, X, Y
   BIT — bit-to-bit AND with A
5. Shift/Rotate
   Instructions: ASL — Arithemetic Shift Left

   LSR — Logical Shift Right

   ROL — ROtate Left

   ROR — ROtate Right

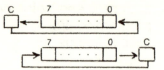

C. PROGRAM CONTROL

1. Test and Branch
   Instructions: BPL — Branch if PLus (N flag clear)
   BMI — Branch if MInus (N flag set)
   BNE — Branch if Not Equal zero (Z flag clear)
   BEQ — Branch if EQual zero (Z flag set)
   BCC — Branch if Carry flag Clear
   BCS — Branch if Carry flag Set
   BVC — Branch if oVerflow flag Clear
   BVS — Branch if oVerflow flag Set
2. Unconditional Jump
   Instruction: JMP
3. Jump to and Return from Subroutine
   Instructions: JSR, RTS
4. Software Break and Return from Interrupt
   Instructions: BRK, RTI

D. MISCELLANEOUS

1. Flag Clear/Set
   Format: CLf — CLear flag f
   SEf - SEt flag f
   Instructions: CLC, CLD, CLI, CLV
   SEC, SED, SEI
2. No OPeration
   Instruction: NOP

Mnemonic	Operation	IMP #=1	IMM #=2	Z-PG. #=2	ABS #=3	ABS.X #=3	ABS.Y #=3	Z-PG.X #=2	Z-PG.Y #=2	(IND,X) #=2	(IND),Y #=2	REL #=2	IND #=3	N	V	-	B	D	I	Z	C
ADC	A+M+C→A		69	65	6D	7D	79	75		61	71			✓	✓					✓	✓
AND	A×M→A		29	25	2D	3D	39	35		21	31			✓						✓	
ASL	C←[7 0]←0	0A		06	0E	iE		16						✓						✓	✓
BCC	branch on C=0											90									
BCS	branch on C=1											B0									
BEQ	branch on Z=1											F0									
BIT	A×M			24	2C									M7	M6					✓	
BMI	branch on N=1											30									
BNE	branch on Z=0											D0									
BPL	branch on N=0											10									
BRK	PC→(S)-, P→(S)-	00															1				
BVC	branch on V=0											50									
BVS	branch on V=1											70									
CLC	0→C	18																			0
CLD	0→D	D8																0			
CLI	0→I	58																	0		
CLV	0→V	B8													0						
CMP	A-M		C9	C5	CD	DD	D9	D5		C1	D1			✓						✓	✓
CPX	X-M		E0	E4	EC									✓						✓	✓
CPY	Y-M		C0	C4	CC									✓						✓	✓
DEC	M-1→M			C6	CE	DE		D6						✓						✓	
DEX	X-1→X	CA												✓						✓	
DEY	Y-1→Y	88												✓						✓	
EOR	A×M→A		49	45	4D	5D	59	55		41	51			✓						✓	
INC	M+1→M			E6	EE	FE		F6						✓						✓	
INX	X+1→X	E8												✓						✓	
INY	Y+1→Y	C8												✓						✓	
JMP	M16→PC				4C								6C								
JSR	PC→(S)-, M16→PC				20																
LDA	M→A		A9	A5	AD	BD	B9	B5		A1	B1			✓						✓	
LDX	M→X		A2	A6	AE		BE		B6					✓						✓	
LDY	M→Y		A0	A4	AC	BC		B4						✓						✓	

111

Mnemonic	Operation	IMP #=1	IMM #=2	Z-PG #=2	ABS #=3	ABS.X #=3	ABS.Y #=3	Z-PG.X #=2	Z-PG.Y #=2	(IND.X) #=2	(IND).Y #=2	REL #=2	IND #=3	N	V	-	B	D	I	Z	C
LSR	0→[7 0]→C	4A		46	4E	5E								0						✓	✓
NOP	PC+1→PC	EA																			
ORA	A∨M→A		09	05	0D	1D	19	15		01	11			✓						✓	
PHA	A→(S)-	48																			
PHP	P→(S)-	08																			
PLA	(S)+→A	68												✓						✓	
PLP	(S)+→P	28												✓	✓		✓	✓	✓	✓	✓
ROL	C←[7 0]←C	2A		26	2E	3E								✓						✓	✓
ROR	C→[7 0]→C	6A		66	6E	7E								✓						✓	✓
RTI	(S)+→P,(S)++→PC	40												✓	✓		✓	✓	✓	✓	✓
RTS	(S)++→PC,S+1→S	60																			
SBC	A-M+C→A		E9	E5	ED	FD	F9	F5		E1	F1			✓	✓					✓	✓
SEC	1→C	38																			1
SED	1→D	F8																1			
SEI	1→I	78																	1		
STA	A→M			85	8D	9D	99	95		81	91										
STX	X→M			86	8E				96												
STY	Y→M			84	8C			94													
TAX	A→X	AA												✓						✓	
TAY	A→Y	A8												✓						✓	
TSX	S→X	BA												✓						✓	
TXA	X→A	8A												✓						✓	
TXS	X→S	9A																			
TYA	Y→A	98												✓						✓	

A   Accumulator
X   X-Index Register
Y   Y-Index Register
P   Processor Status Register
S   Stack Pointer
PC Program Counter
M   Operand in memory

M_{16} 16-bit Operand in Memory
(S)-   Operand Pushed on Stack
(S)--   16-bit Operand Pushed on Stack
(S)+   Operand Popped off Stack
(S)++   16-bit Operand Popped off Stack
+   Add

—   Subtract
∧   AND
∨   OR
⊻   Exclusive OR
No. of Bytes for Instruction

✓   Modified
1   Set to 1
0   Clear to 0
M_7 Memory Bit 7
M_6 Memory Bit 6

SIMPLE MACHINE
LANGUAGE PROGRAMS

Here are a couple of simple machine language programs to get yourself familiar with the instructions and different addressing modes of the 6510 microprocessor.

A. CONVERTING A BINARY BYTE VALUE TO 2 ASCII HEXADECIMAL DIGITS

This program converts a binary value to 2 hexadecimal digits in ASCII values and puts them in a buffer. It illustrates the uses of some data manipulation instructions and the calling of subroutines.

Main conversion program.   BINASC

```
AD 2A C0   binasc   lda binary      ;get binary
48                  pha             ;save it
4A                  lsr a
4A                  lsr a
4A                  lsr a           ;right shift 4 times
4A                  lsr a           ;to get high nibble down
 0 20 C0            jsr hexasc      ;convert to ASCII value
AC 2B C0            ldy bufptr      ;
99 2C C0            sta buff,y      ;put in buffer
68                  iny             ;bump buffer pointer
68                  pla             ;get binary again
29 0F               and #$0f        ;mask to get low nibble
20 20 C0            jsr hexasc      ;convert to ASCII
99 2C C0            sta buff,y      ;put in buffer
C8                  iny
8C 2B C0            sty bufptr      ;update buffer pointer
60                  rts
           ;convert 1 hexadecimal digit to ASCII subroutine
C9 0A      hexasc   cmp #$0a        ;0-9?
90 03               bcc hexal       ;yes,add $30 only
18                  clc             ;no,for A-F
69 07               adc #7          ;add $07 more
           hexal
69 30               adc #$30
60                  rts
           ;data area
           binary   .ds 1
           bufptr   .ds 1
           buff     .ds 256
```

To use 'BINASC', POKE the binary number to be converted into the location defined by BINARY. Call 'BINASC' by using SYS (BINASC) where BINASC = the address of the start of the machine code (e.g. 49152 or $C000).

B. RETRIEVING A VARIABLE-LENGTH MESSAGE WITH AN INDEX

This program retrieves a variable-length message (e.g. error message) from a table of up to 128 messages given its index (e.g. error number). An index table is kept at zero page pointing to the start of each message. The first byte of each message is actually its length.

The two unique index addressing modes of the 6500 family processors are utilized here for illustration purposes

```
AD 2B C0   retriv      lda index         ;get index
0A                      asl a             ;times 2 to access the
AA                      tax               ;correct 2 byte pointer
A1 04                   lda (ixtbl,x)     ;take first byte of message
8D 2C C0                sta length        ;as length of message
            ;set up pointers for retrieving actual message
B5 04                   lda ixtbl,x       ;init pointer at start
85 02                   sta msgptr        ;of desired message
B5 05                   lda ixtbl+1,x     
85 03                   sta msgptr+1      
A0 01                   ldy #1            ;start from actual message text
AE 2D C0                ldx bufptr        ;output buffer pointer
            ;move message to buffer using
            ;indirect index addressing
B1 02      move         lda (msgptr),y    ;retrieve message
9D 2E C0                sta buff,x        ;put in buffer
C8                      iny               
E8                      inx               
CE 2C C0                dec length        ;for its whole length
D0 F8                   bne move          
8E 2D C0                stx bufptr        ;update buffer pointer
60                      rts               
            ;data area
            index       .ds 1             ;index no. (0-127)
            length      .ds 1             ;message length counter
            bufptr      .ds 1             ;buffer pointer
            msgptr      .de 2             ;message pointer (zero page)
            buff        .ds 256           ;256 byte buffer
            ;
            ;index table (zero page)
            ixtbl       .de 4             ;table of addresses
                                          ;of msg1,msg2 and msg3
            ;table of variable length messages
            msg1        .by 9             'i/o error'
            msg2        .by 12            'syntax error'
            msg3        .by 15            'buffer overflow'
```

MON— SIMPLE MACHINE CODE MONITOR

Purpose: to enable the user to examine and change the contents of memory displayed in hex.

When the program is run the user is prompted for a start address. This may be entered in decimal or hex. Hex addresses are indicated by a $ immediately preceding the address, e.g. $D800. Following this, 200 bytes, from the start address on, will be displayed. Cursor control keys move the cursor around the screen as usual. A RETURN keystroke will clear the screen and redisplay the start address prompt. Memory locations are changed by changing the appropriate display. Only legal hex digits will be accepted.

Where there are ROM/RAM overlays the ROM values will be displayed and the RAM values changed unless the ROM is switched out by the user.

```
5 REM MACHINE CODE MONITOR
10 GOTO 900
20 REM DEC TO HEX CONVERSION
30 H$=""
40 V=NR-INT(NR/16)*16
50 H$=H$(V)+H$
60 NR=INT(NR/16)
70 IF NR<>0 THEN 40
80 RETURN
90 REM HEX TO DEC CONVERSION
100 NR=0
110 FOR J=1 TO LEN(NR$)
120 NR=D(ASC(MID$(NR$,J,1))-48)+(NR*16)
    :NEXT:RETURN
160 REM CRSR MOVE LEFT/RIGHT
170 CA=CA+MOVE
180 REM DISABLE CRSR,PRINT,ENABLE CRSR
190 WAIT207,255,1:POKE204,255:POKE205,1:PRINTK$;
    :POKE204,0:RETURN
195 REM CRSR MOVE UP
200 IF CA<SA+8 THEN RETURN
210 CA=CA-8:SM=SM-40:GOSUB 180:RETURN
300 IF CA>SA+191 THEN RETURN
310 CA=CA+8:SM=SM+40:GOSUB 180:RETURN
400 IF SM=2020 THEN RETURN
410 T=SM-1060
420 IF T/40=INT(T/40) THEN CA=CA+1:SM=SM+11
    :K$="▮▮▮▮▮▮▮▮▮▮▮":GOSUB180:RETURN
```
CSRRT times 11
```
430 MOVE=ABS(INT(SM/2)=SM/2)
440 SM=SM+(2*MOVE)+1
```
CSRRT times 3
```
450 T=MOVE*2+1:K$=RIGHT$("▮▮▮",T):GOSUB
    160:RETURN
500 REM CRSR MOVE LEFT
510 IF SM=1031 THEN RETURN
520 T=SM-1031
530 IF T/40=INT(T/40) THEN CA=CA-1:SM=SM-12
    :K$="▮▮▮▮▮▮▮▮▮▮▮▮":GOSUB 180:RETURN
```
CSRLFT times 12

115

```
540 MOVE=( INT( SM/2 )< >SM/2 )
550 SM=SM+( 3*MOVE )-1                    [CSRLFT times 4]
560 T=ABS( MOVE )*3+1:K$=RIGHT$( "████",T):GOSUB
    160:RETURN
600 REM GET VALUE FROM SCREEN
610 POKE204,255:HB=PEEK( SM-1 ):LB=PEEK( SM ):POKE204,0
613 IF HB>127 THEN HB=HB-128
617 IF LB>127 THEN LB=LB-128
620 IF HB<48 THEN NR$=CHR$( 64+HB ):GOTO640
630 NR$=CHR$( HB )
640 IF LB<48 THEN NR$=NR$+CHR$( 64+LB ):GOTO 660
650 NR$=NR$+CHR$( LB )
660 RETURN
700 REM POKE VALUE-2ND DIGIT CHANGED
710 GOSUB 600:GOSUB 90
720 POKECA,NR
730 IF CA=SA+400THEN PRINT"█":RETURN
740 T=( ( CA-SA+1 )/8< >INT( ( CA-SA+1 )/8 ) )
750 IF T THEN K$="██":GOSUB 180:SM=SM+3:CA=CA+1
    :RETURN
                                        [√ CSRRT times 7]
760 SM=SM+11:CA=CA+1:K$=CHR$( 13 )+"████████"
    :GOSUB 180:RETURN
800 REM CONVERT START ADDRESS
810 IF LEFT$( SA$,1 )< >"$" THEN SA=VAL( SA$ ):RETURN
820 NR$=MID$( SA$,2 ):GOSUB 90:SA=NR:RETURN
900 REM SET UP CONVERSION ARRAYS
910 DIM D( 22 )
920 FOR J=0 TO 9:D( J )=J:NEXT
930 FOR J=17 TO 22:D( J )=J-7:NEXT
1110 DIM H$( 15 )
1120 FOR J=0 TO 9:H$( J )=CHR$( 48+J ):NEXT
1130 FOR J=10 TO 15:H$( J )=CHR$( 55+J ):NEXT
1140 REM INITIALIZATION                  [CLR]
1150 PRINT"▨":INPUT "START ADDRESS";SA$:GOSUB 800
1160 CA=SA:SM=1031
1170 FOR J=0 TO 24:PRINT
1180 NR=SA+J*8:GOSUB 20
1190 PRINTRIGHT$( "0000"+H$+"    ",7 );
1200 FOR K=0 TO 7:
1210 NR=PEEK( SA+J+K ):GOSUB 20
    :PRINTRIGHT$( "00"+H$+"   ",4 );
```

116

```
1220 NEXT K,J
1230 REM MAIN LOOP          HOME & CSRRT times 7
1240 PRINT"▬▮▮▮▮▮▮▮";
1250 POKE204,0
1260 GET K$:IF K$="" THEN 1260
1270 IF K$="▯"THEN GOSUB 200:GOTO 1260    CSRUP
1280 IF K$="▨"THEN GOSUB 300:GOTO 1260    CSRDWN
1290 IF K$="▮"THEN GOSUB 400:GOTO 1260    CSRRT
1300 IF K$="▮"THEN GOSUB 500:GOTO 1260    CSRLFT
1310 IF K$=CHR$(13) THEN GOTO 1150
1320 REM CHECK IF LEGAL HEX DIGIT
1330 K=ASC(K$)
1340 IF K<45 OR K>70 THEN 1260
1350 IF K>57 AND K<65 THEN 1260
1360 GOSUB 180
1370 IF SM/2 <> INT(SM/2) THEN SM=SM+1:GOSUB
     600:GOSUB 90:POKECA,NR:GOTO 1260
1380 IF CA=SA+199 THEN K$="▮":GOSUB 180:GOSUB
     600:GOSUB 90:POKECA,NR:GOTO 1260
1390 GOSUB 700:GOTO 1260
2000 PRINT"▯":POKE204,0
2010 PRINT"▨";PEEK(651);PEEK(652);:GOTO 2010
```

117

COMMODORE 64 MEMORY MAP & MANAGEMENT

MEMORY MAP & 'SHADOW ZONES'

As you should know by now, the 6510 processor with a 16-bit address bus has a capability of addressing 64K bytes of memory. For any computer to operate, or almost any, this memory has to be a combination of ROM, RAM and I/O. With a clever design, Commodore 64 actually puts more than 64K of memory into the machine.

Let us examine the memory map and find out how this is achieved. The 64K memory can be divided into 6 zones, 3 of which are 'shadow zones'. In a shadow zone, more than 1 bank of memory exists. These memory banks can be switched in and out under memory management.

Zone	Address	Size	Contents
Zone 6 : E000-FFFF		8K	KERNAL ROM ↔ RAM
Zone 5 : D000-DFFF		4K	I/O / RAM ↔ Character ROM
Zone 4 : C000-CFFF		4K	RAM
Zone 3 : A000-BFFF		8K	BASIC ROM/External ROM ↔ RAM
Zone 2 : 8000-9FFF		8K	RAM/External ROM
Zone 1 : 0000-7FFF		32K	RAM

Commodore 64 Memory Map

ZONE 1 — 32K RAM

The first 32K of memory is RAM and RAM only. No 'shadow' memory is hidden in this zone. However, addresses 0000 and 0001 are overridden by the 6510 internal I/O port registers. Also, remember that Page 1 ($0100 — $01FF) is reserved as the processor stack.

ZONE 2 — 8K RAM/'AUTO-START' EXTERNAL ROM CARTRIDGE

Normally this is a RAM zone but will be overridden by a plug-in ROM cartridge. This external ROM cartridge plugged in can have an 'auto-start' feature to override the usual operating system. The 'auto-start' ROM executes its own codes on power-up if the first nine bytes ($8000 — $8008) are as shown.

	$30	"0"
$8007	$38	"8"
	$CD	"M"
	$C2	"B"
$8004	$C3	"C"
	WSV$_L$	Warm Start
$8002	WSV$_H$	vector
	CSV$_H$	Cold Start
$8000	CSV$_L$	vector

"Auto-start" ROM Header

ZONE 3 — 8K (BASIC ROM/EXTERNAL ROM CARTRIDGE) — RAM

Usually this is the BASIC ROM but will be overridden by the second half of a 16K ROM cartridge plugged in (A 16K plug-in ROM covers Zone 2 and 3). A 'shadow' RAM exists in this zone which can be banked in and out under software control. A processor signal LORAM is used for this purpose. More on this later on.

ZONE 4 — 4K RAM

This 4K of RAM in a higher portion of memory is normally used as a buffer area by the operating system.

ZONE 5 = 4K (I/O / RAM) — CHARACTER ROM

Normally this is the I/O devices' area. Only with memory configuration that does not have any I/O device will RAM appear in this zone. The 'shadow' character ROM can be banked in and out under processor control of signal CHAREN.

ZONE 6 — 8K KERNAL ROM — RAM

Usually this is the KERNAL ROM but the 'shadow' RAM can be switched in and out under software control of processor signal HIRAM.

NOTE: Even when RAM is banked out in case of Zone 3 or Zone 6, a WRITE or POKE operation to a ROM address wil store the data in the 'shadow' RAM. This characteristic allows, for example, a hi-resolution screen to be stored in a 'shadow' RAM area without banking it in and out.

MEMORY MANAGEMENT

Memory management on Commodore 64, in essence, is the selection of banks in particular zones of memory by using some control signals. It is best illustrated in a table:-

Zone	Address	Signal	Level	Access (Bank-in)
3	$A000 — $BFFF (8K)	LORAM	1	BASIC/External ROM
			0	RAM
5	$D000 — $DFFF (4K)	CHAREN	1	I/O / RAM
			0	Character ROM
6	$E000 — $FFFF (8K)	HIRAM	1	KERNAL ROM
			0	RAM

Memory Management Signals (NOTE: All three signals are normally 1)

These control signals are taken from the 6510 internal I/O port which also has 3 other signals that control a cassette. The direction of each line of the port is set up by a bit pattern written into the data direction register (address $0000). A 0 bit designates an input line on the I/O port (address $0001) while a 1 bit corresponds to an output line.

Bit	Data Direction Register ($0000)	I/O Port Control Lines ($0001)
0	1 (output)	LORAM
1	1 (output)	CHAREN
2	1 (output)	HIRAM
3	1 (output)	Cassette write line
4	0 (input)	Cassette switch sense
5	1 (output)	Cassette motor control

6510 Input/Output Port Assignment

SOME MEMORY CONFIGURATIONS

Here are some illustrations of possible memory configurations available on the Commodore 64. The characteristics and main use of each configuration and the levels of control signals that achieve it are listed.

(NOTE: 1 = HIGH, 0 = LOW, X = DON'T CARE)

Standard — 8K ROM BASIC 2.0 and 38K contiguous user RAM

8K KERNAL ROM	LORAM = 1
E000	
4K I/O	HIRAM = 1
D000	
4K RAM (buffer)	CHAREN = 1
C000	
8K BASIC ROM	EXROM = 1
A000	
8K RAM	GAME = 1
8000	
32K RAM (30K user 1K video 1K OS)	
0000	

Enhanced BASIC — 8K BASIC standard ROM and 8K enhanced BASIC
ROM and 32K contiguous RAM

8K KERNAL ROM	LORAM = 1
E000	
4K I/O	HIRAM = 1
D000	
4K RAM (buffer)	CHAREN = 1
C000	
8K BASIC ROM	EXROM = 1
A000	GAME = 0
8K ROM Cartridge (Enhanced BASIC)	
8000	
32K RAM	
0000	

Language ROM — 8K Language ROM (override BASIC) and 40K
contiguous RAM

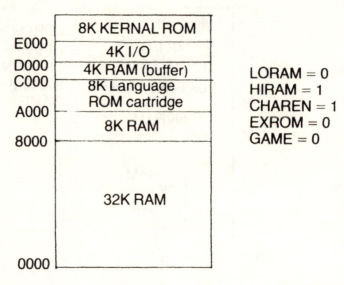

	8K KERNAL ROM
E000	
	4K I/O
D000	
	4K RAM (buffer)
C000	
	8K Language ROM cartridge
A000	
	8K RAM
8000	
	32K RAM
0000	

LORAM = 0
HIRAM = 1
CHAREN = 1
EXROM = 0
GAME = 0

Allocation ROM — 16K application or language ROM and 32K
contiguous RAM.
e.g. word processors, intelligent terminals

	8K KERNAL ROM
E000	
D000	4K I/O
C000	4K RAM (buffer)
	16K Rom Cartridge
8000	
	32K RAM
0000	

LORAM = 1
HIRAM = 1
CHAREN = 1
EXROM = 0
GAME = 0

ULTIMAX Video Game — 16K ROM and 4K RAM only

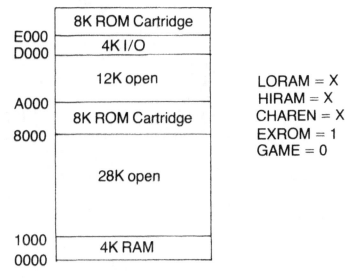

8K ROM Cartridge
E000
D000   4K I/O

12K open
A000

8K ROM Cartridge
8000

28K open

1000
0000   4K RAM

LORAM = X
HIRAM = X
CHAREN = X
EXROM = 1
GAME = 0

Softload Language 52K contiguous RAM for softload languages, user RAM, I/O devices and I/O drive routines, e.g. CP/M

8K KERNAL ROM
E000
D000   4K I/O
C000   4K ROM

16K RAM
8000

32K RAM

0000

LORAM = 0
HIRAM = 1
CHAREN = 1
EXROM = X
GAME = 1

64K RAM — I/O devices must be banked in for any I/O operation

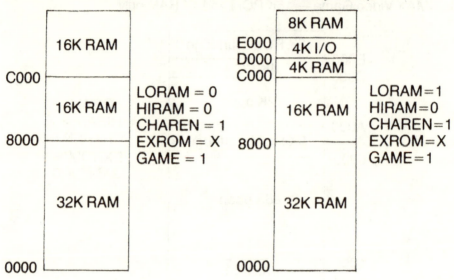

PROGRAM ENTRY

There are 3 common methods of entering machine code programs on the Commodore 64.

1. BASIC STATEMENTS

This method is suitable for simple and short machine code routines used within a BASIC program. First of all, the routine has to be assembled, usually by hand. Each code is converted to its decimal value (an unfamiliar numbering system to a machine language programmer). Then the codes are stored in BASIC DATA statments. A simple READ and POKE loop will set up the machine code routine at a specific location. Subsequent SYS or USR statements can use this routine.

This is the cheapest method because no additional purchase of software is required. However, the amount of time required to debug or modify the code will increase drastically with the size of the routine. Imagine typing a 500 byte program in decimal values or several scores of DATA statements and then having to locate a typing or conversion mistake.
Example:

```
5 RESTORE : M = 12 * 4096 : REM $C000
6 READ X : IF X <> −1 THEN POKE M, X : M=M+1, GOTO  6
10 Initialization of formal basic
.
.
.
1000 DATA 32, 207,255,157,0,193,232,201,13,246,96, −1
```

Notes:-

a) The use of delimiter −1 avoids the problem of having to count the numbers of bytes as in a FOR...NEXT loop.

b) Subsequent running of this BASIC program should start at line 10. This eliminates the time-consuming READ and POKE process to set up the machine code registers (of course, self-modifying codes are always forbidden!).

2. MACHINE LANGUAGE MONITOR

A ROM cartridge called 64MON is provided by Commodore to let you
a) enter machine code programs in Hexadecimal codes or Mnemonic forms
b) assemble and disassemble machine language
c) debug machine code programs
d) save and load machine code programs.

A monitor of this kind is recommended for any serious machine language programmer. With 64MON, you can enter a machine code routine by specifying the starting address and then the instructions.

Example:

```
A C000 JSR $FFCF
A C003 STA $C100, X
A C006 INX
A C007 CMP #$0D
A C009 BNE $C000
A C00A RTS
```

3. EDITOR/ASSEMBLER PACKAGE

An editor/assembler allows you, at the very least, to use label references in programs and save source programs instead of object codes. A more sophisticated package can have the following features:-
— macro, conditional and/or interactive assembly
— symbol table and cross reference
— formatted assembly listing
— object modules linking and relocation
— run-time debug aids

With an editor/assembler, you can write much better documented assembly language programs.

Example:-

```
CHRIN    =     $FFCF       ; input 1 character routine
LINEBUF  =     $C100       ; input line buffer
CR       =     13          ; [RETURN] character
         *=    $C00        ; code starting address
GETLINE: JSR   CHRIN       ;input 1 character
         STA   LINEBUF, X  ; put character in line buffer
         INX
```

```
CMP   #CR        ; is it [RETURN] character?
BNE   GETLINE    ; NO — get next charcter
RTS              ; exit only if whole line input
```

PROGRAM EXECUTION

A machine language program can be executed by calling it in a BASIC program or directly run under a machine language monitor. Some of the system handling routines can be substituted by user written ones with careful modification of the vectors.

1. BASIC CONTROL PROGRAM

A BASIC porgram can use machine code routines as subroutines. These subroutines must end with a 'RTS' instruction to return control to the BASIC calling program. There are 2 ways of calling machine language subroutines in BASIC.

a) SYS [addr] statement

This BASIC statement enters a machine language subroutine at address [addr]. Execution continues with the next BASIC statement on return. Parameters can be passed by putting them in commonly known memory locations. This method allows simple and efficient interface between BASIC and machine language programs. Multiple parameters and several machine code subroutines are handled with ease.

b) USR ([x]) Function

This BASIC function calls a machine language subroutine whose entry point is stored at address 785, 786 (conventional low, high byte order). The parameter [x] is passed by putting its value in the Floating Point Accumulator #1. On return, BASIC will take the value in the floating point accumulator as the value of the function. This method is more suitable for routines that pass a single parameter only, especially with floating point numbers. Be careful to set up the correct entry point at 785 and 786 before calling this function when you have more than one machine code subroutine.

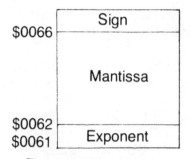

Floating Point Accumulator #1

2. MACHINE LANGUAGE MONITOR

With 64MON, you can execute a machine code routine by specifying its starting address. The routine should end with a 'BRK' instruction to return control the the monitor.
Example:
G C000
By setting up breakpoints, memory and registers can be examined at critical points. The routine can then be resumed with or without any alteration. This makes debugging of the machine language program easier.

3. SUBSTITUTION OF SYSTEM HANDLING ROUTINES

For those system routines which are called via their indirect vectors in RAM, they can be easily substituted by modifying their corresponding vectors to point to the user written routines.
Such user routines must end in the same way as their system equivalents — either with a 'RTS' or a 'RTI' instruction. Normally, you want to do something extra before transferring the control back to the standard routine. Therefore a 'JMP' instruction will be more frequently used here.
Here are some system handling routines that can be substituted.
a) BASIC Interpreter Routines
— e.g. tokenize keywords, LIST, print error messages and evaluate tokens, etc.
The vector table resides at $0300 — $030B
b) KERNAL Input/Output Routines
— e.g. OPEN/CLOSE, LOAD/SAVE, CHRIN/CHROUT, etc
The vector table resides at $031A — $0333
c) Processor Interrupt Handlers
—e.g. hardware interrupt request (IRQ), non-maskable interrupt (NMI), software interrupt instruction (BRK)
The vector table resides at $0314 — $0319.
(NOTE: IRQ interrupts every 1/50 of a second (1/60 in U.S.A) and the KERNAL makes use of this to update the time (TI, TI$) and scan the keyboard. Make sure you return to the system handler unless you intend otherwise. Disable IRQ before you modify its vector)
d) 'Wedge' New Commands
— By detouring from the CHRGET (get next BASIC byte) routine at $73
— $8A, new commands can be added. If all new commands begin with a common character (@ is a popular choice), 'wedging' interpretation will be faster. Commands that do not start with '@' are passed back to the standard handling routine; those that do start with '@' are searched and executed by the user routine.
e)Keyboard Entry Routines
— e.g. keyboard table setup and decode, INPUT routine
Keys can be redefined according to user requirement.

SOME COMMODORE 64 USEFUL ROUTINES

A. PAUSING 'LIST' OUTPUT

A very short machine language routine can add to the Commodore 64 a highly desirable feature on the LIST program command. The continuous scrolling of text lines on the screen is usually too fast for the human eyes. It would be nice to pause the output by holding down the shift key and be able to freeze it by pressing the shift-lock key. The following routine does just that.

```
                shflag      .de  $028   ;($01=shift-key pressed)
                slist       .de  $a71a  ;system LIST tokens routine
                            .ba  $c000  ;pause routine starts at $c000
C000 A5 28      wait        lda  shflag ;shift key pressed?
C002 D0 FC                  bne  wait   ;yes, wait for release
C004 68                     pla         ;no restore token
C005 4C 1A A7               jmp  slist  ;LIST token
```

This is an example of substituting BASIC interpreter routines — the LIST tokens handler. By modifying the vector at $0306, this coding of pause check can be inserted before the actual printing of tokens. If we have the above codes at $C000, we can enable the pause feature by POKE 774, 0 :POKE 775, 192 (i.e. $C000 — $0306).

B. PROGRAMMING FUNCTION KEYS

Each of the Commodore 64's eight function keys can be used to represent a series of keystrokes as entered from the keyboard.

The operating system uses a keyboard buffer queue to store any key entered from the keyboard. The system IRQ interrupt handler puts entered keys at the end of the queue while the BASIC interpreter takes them off the queue in a first-in-first-out (FIFO) order. If a user interrupt routine puts on the queue a string of pre-defined chracters when a function key is pressed, the system will be deceived to think that the string was actually typed on the keyboard.

This method of programming function keys can illustrate the technique of substituting a system interrupt handling routine. The following simple example will put "LIST [RETURN]" on the keyboard buffer queue when [f1] key is hit.

```
                        .ba  $c000
          cr            .de  13          ;RETURN character
          ndx           .de  $c6         ;no. of characters in
                                            keyboard buffer queue
          keyd          .de  $0277       ;keyboard buffer queue
                                            (10 bytes long)
          cinv          .de  $0314       ;IRQ interrupt vector in RAM
          sirq          .de  $ea31       ;system IRQ handling routine
          scnkey        .de  $ff9f       ;scan keyboard and put key
                                            entered onto queue

          ;set up to override system IRQ handler with user routine
78        init          sei             ;IRQ must be disabled during
a9 0d                   lda  #l,uirq     ;modification of its vector
8d 14 03                sta  cinv
a9 c0                   lda  #h,uirq
8d 15 03                sta  cinv+1
58                      cli
60                      rts
          ;user IRQ handler(executed every 1/50th of a second)
20 9f ff  uirq          jsr  scnkey      ;scan keyboard
a6 c6                   ldx  ndx
f0 16                   beq  exit        ;exit if no key
ca                      dex              ;point at last key in queue
bd 77 02                lda  keyd,x
c9 85                   cmp  #$85        ;[F1]?
d0 0e                   bne  exit        ;no, do nothing
a0 ff                   ldy  #255        ;yes, put predefined string
c8        put           iny              ;onto keyboard buffer queue
e8                      inx
b9 2d c0                lda  string,y
9d 77 02                sta  keyd,x
d0 f6                   bne  put         ;string terminated by byte 0
86 c6                   stx  ndx         ;update no. of bytes in queue
4c 31 ea  exit          jmp  sirq        ;resume with system IRQ handler
          ;user definable string of keys
4c 49 53  string        .by  'LIST'      cr 0
54
0d 00
```

With the machine codes residing from $C000 upwards, the initialization
routine can be activated by SYS 12*4096.

C. RECOVERING "NEWed" PROGRAM

This program we will use will also serve to show how additional
commands can be 'wedged' into the BASIC operating system. Below is a
listing of an operating system routine 'CHRGET' that we will wedge our
routine into.

```
0073 E6 7A        CHRGET      INC TXTPTR ; get next byte
0075 DO 02                    BNE CHRGOT
0077 E6 7B                    INC TXTPTR+1
0079 AD ?? ??     CHRGOT      LDA ???? ; get current byte
007C C9 3A                    CMP #$3A
007E NO 0A                    BCS CHRET ; ignore ASCII   '9'
0080 C9 20                    CMP #$20
0082 F0 EF                    BEQ CHRGET ; skip space characters
0084 38                       SEC
0085 E9 30                    SBC #$30
0087 38                       SEC
0088 E9 D0                    SBC #$D0
008A 60           CHRET       RTS
```

NOTE:
Locations $7A and $7B are used as TXTPTR which points at the current byte in the BASIC text buffer to be interpreted. This routine is kept in RAM so that it can modify ????, the address of the current byte, continually.

We will make use of the fact that CHRGET resides in RAM by wedging our routine into CHRGET. To use this routine, it must have already been loaded before the NEW command was executed. To recover a NEWed program, simply type @OLD.

```
10                 .os
20                 .ba $c000
30 CHRGET          .de $73        ;get next BASIC byte routine
40 CHRGOT          .de $79        ;get current BASIC byte routine
50 TXTPTR          .de $7a        ;current BASIC byte pointer
60 IERROR          .de $0300      ;vector of print error message routine
70                 .ba $c000
80 ; DETOUR FROM CHRGET
90                 LDX #2
100 DETR1          LDA JCODE,X    ;replace 1st instruction of CHRGET
110                STA CHRGET,X   ;with 'jump wedge'
120                DEX
130                BPL DETR1
140                RTS
150 JCODE          JMP WEDGE      ;jump instruction codes
160 XSAVE          .DS 1
170 ; CHECK FOR WEDGE COMMANDS
180 WEDGE
190                INC TXTPTR     ;POINT AT NEXT BYTE
200                BNE WEDG1
210                INC TXTPTR+1
220 WEDG1          STX XSAVE
230                TSX
240                SEC
```

```
250               LDA $0101,X
260               SBC #$8C
270               ADC $0102,X      ;was CHRGET called from
280               SBC #$A4         ;the direct mode?
290               BNE WEDG9        ;ignore wedge commands
300                                ;from other modes
310               JSR CHRGOT
320               CMP #'@           ;wedge command identifier?
330               BEQ WDGCMD       ;yes,dispatch command
340 WEDG9         LDX XSAVE        ;no restore X
350               JMP CHRGOT       ;return
360 ; dispatch wedge commands
370 ;(for the simplicity of this example
380 ; proper handling should involve storing
390 ; all valid commands in a table and
400 ; searching the input command through
410 ; the table).
420 WDGCMD        JSR CHRGET       ;get next byte
430               CMP #'O           ;old?
440               BEQ RECOVR       ;yes,recovery routine
450               CMP #'R
460               BEQ RECOVR
470               LDX #$0B         ;if invalid command
480               JMP (IERROR)     ;print syntax error
490 ; RECOVER "NEWED" PROGRAM
500 TXTTAB        .de $2b          ;pointer :start of basic
510 VARTAB        .de $2d          ;pointer :start of basic variables
520 ARYTAB        .de $2f          ;pointer :start of basic arrays
530 STREND        .de $31          ;pointer :end of basic arrays
540 PTR           .de $2d
550 TEMP          .de $2f
560 RECOVR
570               LDY #3           ;disgard next-line pointer & line no.
580 RCVR1         INY
590               LDA (TXTTAB),Y   ;search for line delimiter
600               BNE RCVR1        ;(<$00) of first line
610               TYA
620               SEC              ;+1 to point to 2nd line
630               ADC TXTTAB
640               LDY #0
650               STA (TXTTAB),Y   ;rectify next-line pointer
660                                ;for first line
670               STA $2D          ;init temp work pointer
680               INY
690               LDA $2C
700               STA (TXTTAB),Y
710               STA $2E
720 ;trace next line until end of program text
730               LDY #0
740 RCVR2         LDA ($2D),Y
750               STA $2F
760               INY              ;position to address high
770               LDA ($2D),Y
780               TAX
790               ORA $2F          ;link address=$0000?
800               BEQ RCVR3        ;yes,end of program
810               STX $2E          ;no,trace next link
820               LDA $2F
```

131

```
830              STA $2D
840              DEY              ;reposition to address low
850              BEQ RCVR2        ;always branch
860 ;correct all BASIC pointers
870 RCVR3        CLC
880              LDA $2D
890              ADC #2           ;position right after end of program
900              STA $2D          ;for start of variables
910              STA $2F          ;for start of arrays
920              STA $31          ;for end of arrars
930              LDA $2E
940              ADC #0
950              STA $2E
960              STA $30
970              STA $32
980              LDX #$80         ;print READY
990              JMP (IERROR)     ;& return to BASIC
1600             .EN
```

```
80 REM WEDGE THAT ADDS COMMAND @OLD
90 REM WHICH RESTORES NEWED PROGRAMS
100 FOR I=0 TO 139:READ A :POKE 49152+I,A:NEXT
110 SYS 49152
120 DATA192,2,189,11,192,149,115,202
130 DATA16,248,96,76,15,192,255,230
140 DATA122,208,2,230,123,142,14,192
150 DATA136,56,189,1,1,233,140,125
160 DATA2,1,233,164,208,7,32,121
170 DATA0,201,64,240,6,174,14,192
180 DATA76,121,0,32,115,0,201,79
190 DATA240,9,201,82,240,5,162,11
200 DATA108,0,3,160,3,200,177,43
210 DATA208,251,152,56,101,43,160,0
220 DATA145,43,133,45,200,165,44,145
230 DATA43,133,46,160,0,177,45,133
240 DATA47,200,177,45,170,5,47,240
250 DATA8,134,46,165,47,133,45,136
260 DATA240,235,24,165,45,105,2,133
270 DATA45,133,47,133,49,165,46,105
280 DATA0,133,46,133,48,133,50,162
290 DATA128,108,0,3
```

132

COMMODORE 64 KERNAL

CONCEPTS OF KERNAL AND OPERATING SYSTEM

A microprocessor, no matter how large its instruction set is and no matter how fast it can run, will get nowhere without a well-knit piece of software that supervises it. This supervisory program is known as an OPERATING SYSTEM. The operating system accepts what you type on the keyboard; echoes it on the monitor; prints an error message if it does not understand what you typed; executes your command if it makes sense; loads a program from disk drive if necessary; prints something on the printer if required; ... In other words, the operating system co-ordinates and manages all resources of the computer to be at your service.

The operating system has a large collection of routines that perform system initializations, memory management and all kinds of input/output. These routines are usually highly hardware dependent which means different routines have to be written for different devices. From a user point of view, you want to be able to use these routines without worrying about what hardware you are dealing with. Most microcomputer manufacturers prepare a list of callable system routines with their addresses and methods of calling. The problem arises when a later version of the operating system is released; all these entry points will be different. Old software which made use of these routines is no longer compatible.

Commodore 64 has solved this problem by storing all the entry points of the supported system routines in a Jump Table called KERNAL. This jump table is located on the last page of memory, in the KERNAL ROM. The entries of this table are well documented and will remain unchanged in future ROM releases. Any individual system routine can be modified and relocated inside the ROM. However, such a change will be 'transparent' to the user program as long as the jump pointer in the KERNAL has been updated.

Example :-

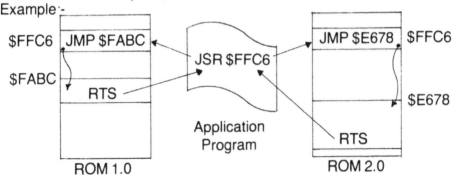

The application program will run just as well on both ROM versions.

POWER-UP INITIALIZATIONS

On power-up, the KERNAL performs a series of self-tests and system initializations. The sequence of activities is outlined below:-

1. For the 6510 processor, the Stack Pointer is reset to $FF and the Decimal Mode Flag is cleared.

2. Location $8004 — $8008 are examined. If an 'auto-start' ROM header is found, control is passed to the 'auto-start' ROM using the vector at $8000. Otherwise, normal power-up sequence continues.

3. I/O ports and devices are initialized
— CIA#1 to scan keyboard, joystick, paddle and light pen
— CIA#1 to activate real-time clock
— CIA#2 to initialize Serial Bus
— CIA#2 to reset User/RS-232 port
— SID to clear all voices
— 6510 I/O port to select memory configuration for BASIC mode
— 6510 I/O port to turn off cassette motor.

4. RAM test is carried out from $0300 upwards. The top memory pointer is determined by the first non-RAM location encountered. The bottom memory pointer is always set to $0800. The screen memory always starts at $0400.

5. All I/O vectors, pointers, flags and variables in RAM are initialized.

6. The screen is cleared and all the screen editor variables reset. Control is passed to BASIC using the vector at $A000.
Next time if you notice a slight delay when turning the power on, you will know that it is working very hard to get all these things straightened out.

USING KERNAL ROUTINES

For you to use the KERNAL routines, you must:-
— find out the right one to use and its entry point address
— call preparatory routine, if necessary
— pass parameters in communication registers,
— call the routine
— handle any return error (indicated by Carry Flag set)
— save and restore registers affected by the routine, if necessary

SOME USEFUL KERNAL ROUTINES

Routine	Address	Function	Preparatory Routines	Communications Registers	Registers Affected
User Interface					
1. CHRIN	$FFCF	Input 1 Character (from keyboard)	—	.A = input character	.X,.Y
2. CHROUT	$FFD2	Output 1 Character (to Screen)	—	.A = output character	—
3. GETIN	$FFE4	Get 1 Character from Keyboard Queue	—	.A = character removed = 0 if none	.X,.Y
4. PLOT	$FFF0	Read/Set Cursor Position	—	C flag = 1 read = 0 set .X = row(0-24) .Y = column(0-39)	.A
storage I/O					
5. SETLFS	$FFBA	Set Up Logical File No. First Address (Device No.) and Second Address (Command) of Device	—	.A = logical file no. .X = device no. .Y = command = $FF if no command	—
6. SETNAM	$FFBD	Set Up File Name	—	.A = length of filename .X = filename address (low) .Y = filename address (high)	—
7. LOAD	$FFD5	Load/Verify Memory from Device	SETLFS SETNAM	.A = 0 load = 1 verify	.X,.Y
8. SAVE	$FFD8	Save Memory to Device	SETLFS SETNAM	.A = page-zero address of start SAVE pointer .X = end SAVE pointer address (low) .Y = end SAVE pointer address (high)	

1. CHRIN — INPUT 1 CHARACTER (FROM KEYBOARD)

When this routine is initially called, the cursor will blink and input a line of characters terminated with a carriage return. The routine will return with the first character in .A. Subsequent calls will retrieve the characters already input one by one. Detection of a carriage return means the whole input line has been retrieved. A subsequent call will initiate the cursor blinking and line input again.

2. CHROUT — OUTPUT 1 CHARACTER (TO SCREEN)

A character whose ASCII value is in the .A is printed on the screen and the cursor advances.

3. GETIN — GET 1 CHARACTER FROM KEYBOARD QUEUE

Any key pressed on the keyboard is detected by the system IRQ interrupt handler. Its ASCII code will be stored in a keyboard buffer queue which can hold up to 10 characters. When called, this routine will remove the first character from the queue. If there is no character in the queue, a byte zero will be returned in the .A.

4. PLOT — READ/SET CURSOR POSITION

This routine can read/set the current cursor position when called with the Carry Flag set/clear accordingly .X stores the row number (0 — 24) and Y stores the column number (0 — 39).

5. SETLFS — SET LOGICAL FILE NUMBER, FIRST AND SECOND ADDRESS OF DEVICE

This routine assigns a logical file number to a physical device (device number 0 — 31). The secondary address or command of the device is also declared here. There are a number of reserved device numbers for the Commodore 64:-

Device number	Device
0	Keyboard
1	Cassette
2	RS-232 Device
3	Screen
4	Serial Bus Printer
5	Serial Bus Disk Drive

.A is used to pass the logical file number .X the device number and .Y the command. If no command is required, put $FF in .Y.

6. SETNAM — SET UP FILE NAME

This routine sets up a file name for the LOAD or SAVE routine .A is used to pass the length of the file name and .X and .Y contain the address of the file name (.X = low order, .Y = high order address). If no file name is necessary, .A stores a zero showing a file name of null length.

7. LOAD — LOAD/VERIFY MEMORY FROM DEVICE

When called with a zero in .A, this routine loads a file from device into memory. When called with a one in .A, this routine verifies a file from device against the corresponding contents in the memory.

8. SAVE — SAVE MEMORY TO DEVICE

This routine saves a contiguous portion of memory onto a device file. The start address of the memory to be saved is stored in a page-zero pointer. The .A is used to pass the page-zero address of this start pointer. The .X and .Y are used to pass the end address (in low, high order)

SIMPLE PROGRAMS THAT CALL KERNAL ROUTINES

A. PLOT USING GRAPHICS CHARACTERS

This program plots anywhere on the screen using different graphics characters. Three KERNAL routines are called — CHROUT, GETIN and PLOT.

Call 'plot' from BASIC by typing SYS 49152.
Plot instructions:

[f1] = up
[f3] = right
[f5] = left
[f7] = down
▬ to ◧ = graphics characters
〈space〉 = blank
RUN/STOP = End plot

```
 10                 .os
 20                 .ba $c000
 30 chrout          .de $ffd2
 40 getin           .de $ffe4
 50 plot            .da $fff0
 60 shape           .de $26        ;shape char to plot
 70 xsave           .de $27
 80 ysave           .de $28
 90 blnsw           .de $cc        ;cursor blink flag
100 rptflg          .de $028a      ;repeat key flag
110 ;
120 ;
130 ;initialize screen
140 ;
150 plotg           lda #$93
160                 jsr chrout     ;clear screen
170                 lda #0
180                 sta *blnsw     ;blink cursor
190                 lda #$80
200                 sta rptflg     ;enable repeat
210                 ldx #12        ;init cursor
220                 ldy #19        ;at screen centre
230                 lda #$77
240 upshp           sta *shape     ;update shape
250 ;
260 ;
270 ;print shape char
280 ;
290 outshp
```

```
300             stx *xsave      ;save x,y
310             sty *ysave
320             clc
330             jsr plot        ;set cursor pos.
340             lda *shape
350             jsr chrout      ;print shape
360             lda #$9d        ;backspace
370             jsr chrout
380 ;
390 ;wait for key input
400 ;
410 inkey
420             jsr getin
430             ldx *xsave      ;restore x,y
440             ldy *ysave
450             cmp #0
460             beq inkey       ;no key
470 ;exit if <stop>
480             cmp #3
490             beq exit
500 ;blank if <space>
510             cmp #$20
520             beq upshp
530 ;cursor up if <f1>
540             cmp #$85
550             beq up
560 ;cursor right if <f3>
570             cmp #$86
580             beq right
590 ;cursor left if <f5>
600             cmp #$87
610             beq left
620 ;cursor down if <f7>
630             cmp #$88
640             beq down
650 ;if not graphics char
660 ;($a0-$df)
670 ;then ignore
680             cmp #$a0
690             bcc inkey
700             cmp #$e0
710             bcs inkey
```

```
720 ;update shape char
730              jmp upshp
740 ;
750 ;
760 ;cursor movement
770 ;
780 up           dex              ;dec row
790              cpx #$ff
800              bne up1
810              ldx #24
820 up1          jmp outshp
830 ;
840 down         inx              ;inc row
850              cpx #25
860              bne down1
870              ldx #0
880 down1        jmp outshp
890 ;
900 right        iny              ;inc col
910              cpy #40
920              bne right1
930              ldy #0
940 right1       jmp outshp
950 ;
960 left         dey              ;dec col
970              cpy #$ff
980              bne left1
990              ldy #39
1000 left1       jmp outshp
1610 ;
1620 ;exit to basic
1630 ;
1640 exit         lda #$93
1650              jsr chrout
1660 ;clear screen
1670              rts
1680              .en
PLOT

100 FOR I=0 TO 131:READ A:POKE49152+I,A:NEXT
110 SYS49152
120 DATA169,147,32,210,255,169,0,133
```

139

```
130 DATA204,169,128,141,138,2,162,12
140 DATA160,19,169,119,133,38,134,39
150 DATA132,40,24,32,240,255,165,38
160 DATA32,210,255,169,157,32,210,255
170 DATA32,228,255,166,39,164,40,201
180 DATA0,240,245,201,3,240,71,201
190 DATA32,240,217,201,133,240,23,201
200 DATA134,240,39,201,135,240,45,201
210 DATA136,240,21,201,160,144,217,201
220 DATA224,176,213,76,20,192,202,224
230 DATA255,208,2,162,24,76,22,192
240 DATA32,224,25,208,2,162,0,76
250 DATA2,192,200,192,40,208,2,160
260 DATA0,76,22.192,136,192,255,208
270 DATA2,160,39,76,22,192,169,147
280 DATA32,210,255.96
```

Graphics Using Machine Code

The following programs enable the BASIC programmer simple access to extended graphics facilities such as high resolution plotting. When used creatively these programs can produce quite impressive displays on your Commodore 64.

Graphics.asm is an assembly listing of a program that provides the BASIC programmer with access to graphics commands. These commands, whilst being very useful, also serve as a demonstration of assembly language programming. They enable the programmer to set up a bit mapped screen with one SYS statement, and also to plot points by specifying X and Y co-ordinates. Resourceful programmers will be able to incorporate these routines into their own line drawing and circle drawing programs.

Graphics.bas is BASIC program which reads the assembly code into memory. It also demonstrates the correct use of the assembly routines. Graphics.asm consists of two main routines, HIRES and PLOTXY, as well as several subroutines. HIRES is an excellent example of changing video banks, screens and character sets as well as clearing blocks of memory. PLOTXY is the routine that handles the plotting of points. It calls the routine PARAMS to obtain the X and Y co-ordinates. PARAMS in turn calls many subroutines that reside in the BASIC operating system. The correct use of these routines is shown in the assembly listing.

PLOT, the routine that actually plots the points in memory uses the following formula to determine the address of the byte to be changed.

140

ROW = INT (Y / 8)
COL = INT (X / 8)
LINE = Y AND 7
BIT = 7 − (X AND 7)
ADDRESS = BASE + ROW * 320 + COL * 8 + LINE
where base is the address of the start of the bit map.

The correct bit within the byte is set as follows:-
POKE ADDRESS, PEEK (ADDRESS) OR 2 ↑ BIT
NOTE: the assembly program uses an array containing the values of
2 ↑ BIT.

GRAPHICS ASM

```
          .os                 ;store object code in memory
          .ba $c000           ;begin assembly at $c000 (49152)
tbase     .de $fb             ;variable: pointer to bit map base
;
;
params    jsr $aefa           ;check for bracket
          jsr $ad8a           ;evaluate formula
          jsr $b7f7           ;convert to 16 bit number
          lda $14
          sta newcol          ;x pos. low
          lda $15
          sta newcol+1        ;x pos. high
          jsr $aefd           ;check for comma
          jsr $b79e           ;get 8 bit number
          stx newrow          ;y pos.
          jsr $aef7           ;check for right bracket
          rts
;
;
plot      lda rowcrs          ;get row
          lsr a
          lsr a
          lsr a               ;divide by 8
          sta trow            ;temp row
          lda colcrs
          sta tcol            ;temp column
          lda colcrs+1
          lsr a               ;divide column by 8
          ror tcol
          lsr a
          ror tcol
          lsr a
          ror tcol
          sta tcol+1
          lda rowcrs
          and #7
          sta line            ; offset in row
          lda colcrs
          and #7
          sta bit
          lda #7
          sec
```

141

```
                sbc bit
                sta bit         ;of
                lda #0
                sta *tbase      ;start of screen (low byte)
                lda #$60
                sta *tbase+1    ;start of screen (high byte)
                ldx trow
                beq p1
p3              inc *tbase+1    ; add 256 to screen address
                lda *tbase
                clc
                adc #64         ;add 64 to screen address ( ie 320)
                sta *tbase
                bcc p2
                inc *tbase+1
p2              dex
                bne p3
p1              lda tcol
                asl a
                asl a
                asl a           ;multiply column by 8
                bcc p8
                inc *tbase+1
                clc
p8              adc *tbase
                sta *tbase
                bcc p9
                inc *tbase+1
p9              lda *tbase
                clc
                adc line        ; add row offset
                sta *tbase
                bcc p4
                inc *tbase+1    ;tbase and tbase+1 contain byte address
p4              ldx bit         ;offset into byte
                ldy #0
                lda (tbase),y
                ora ortab,x     ;set proper bit to 1
                sta (tbase),y
                rts
;
;
hires           jsr setbank     ;set video bank
                jsr setchbase   ;set bit map base
                jsr setscreen   ;set screen (bit map color data)
                jsr clrbit      ;clear bit map memory
                jsr clrscreen   ;set bit map color data
                lda $d011
                ora #32
                sta $d011       ;turn on bit map
                lda #0
                sta oldrow      ;set oldrow and oldcol
                sta oldcol
                sta oldrow      ;set oldrow and oldcol
                sta oldcol
                sta oldcol+1
                rts
;
;
```

142

```
setbank     lda $dd02
            ora #3
            sta $dd02       ; set to outputs
            lda $dd00
            and #252
            ora #2          ;set bank 1
            sta $dd00
            rts
;
;
setchbase   lda $d018
            and #240
            ora #8          ;set char base to $2000
                            (ie bit map at $6000)
            sta $d018
            rts
;
;
setscreen   lda $d018
            and #15
            ora #112        ;set screen to $1c00
                            (ie screen address is $5c00
            sta $d018
            rts
;
;
clrscreen   lda #16         ;clear screen data(ie bit map color data)
            ldx #0          ;foreground color =white,background=black
clr         sta $5c00,x
            sta $5d00,x
            sta $5e00,x
            sta $5f00,x
            dex
            bne clr
            rts
;
;
clrbit      lda #$60        ;clears memory from $6000 to $7fff)
            sta *tbase+1
            lda #0
            sta *tbase
            ldy #0
clb         sta (tbase),y
            dey
            bne clb
            inc *tbase+1
            ldx *tbase+1
            cpx #$80
            bne clb
            rts
;
;
plotxy      jsr params      ; get x and y
            lda newrow
            cmp #200        ;legal row?
            bcc xy1
            rts
xy1         lda newcol
            cmp #64         ;legal column
```

143

```
            bcc  xy2
            lda  newcol+1
            beq  xy2
            rts
xy2         lda  newrow          ;update variables
            sta  rowcrs
            sta  oldrow
            lda  newcol
            sta  colcrs
            sta  oldcol
            lda  newcol+1
            sta  oldcol+1
            sta  colcrs+1
            jsr  plot            ;plot point
            rts
;
ortab       .by  1               2 4 8 16 32 64 128
newcol      .ds  2               ;contains new column
newrow      .ds  1               ;contains new row
oldrow      .ds  1               ;contains old row
oldcol      .ds  2               ;contains old column
rowcrs      .ds  1               ;tempory row
colcrs      .ds  2               ;tempory column
trow        .ds  1               ;tempory row
tcol        .ds  2               ;tempory column
line        .ds  1               ;offset into character
bit         .ds  1               ;offset into byte
            .en
```

GRAPHICS BAS

```
 90 REM READ MACHINE CODE INTO ADDRESS 49152
    ONWARDS
100 FOR I=0 TO 345:READ A:POKE 49152+I,A:NEXT
110 GOTO600
120 DATA32,250,174,32,138,173,32,247
130 DATA183,165,20,141,90,193,165,21
140 DATA141,91,193,32,253,174,32,158
150 DATA183,142,92,193,32,247,174,96
160 DATA173,96,193,74,74,74,141,99
170 DATA193,173,97,193,141,100,193,173
180 DATA98,193,74,110,100,193,74,110
190 DATA100,193,74,110,100,193,141,101
200 DATA193,173,96,193,41,7,141,102
210 DATA193,173,97,193,41,7,141,103
220 DATA193,169,7,56,237,103,193,141
230 DATA103,193,169,0,133,251,169,96
240 DATA133,252,174,99,193,240,16,230
250 DATA252,165,251,24,105,64,133,251
260 DATA144,2,230,252,202,208,240,173
270 DATA100,193,10,10,10,144,3,230
280 DATA252,24,101,251,133,251,144,2
```

144

```
290 DATA230,252,165,251,24,109,102,193
300 DATA133,251,144,2,230,252,174,103
310 DATA193,160,0,177,251,29,82,193
320 DATA145,251,96,32,198,192,32,217
330 DATA192,32,228,192,32,3,193,32
340 DATA239,192,173,17,208,9,32,141
350 DATA17,208,169,0,141,93,193,141
360 DATA94,193,141,95,193,96,173,2
370 DATA221,9,3,141,2,221,173,0
380 DATA221,41,252,9,2,141,0,221
390 DATA96,173,24,208,41,240,9,8
400 DATA141,24,208,96,173,24,208,41
410 DATA15,9,112,141,24,208,96,169
420 DATA16,162,0,157,0,92,157,0
430 DATA93,157,0,94,157,0,95,202
440 DATA208,241,96,169,96,133,252,169
450 DATA0,133,251,160,0,145,251,136
460 DATA208,251,230,252,166,252,224,128
470 DATA208,243,96,32,0,192,173,92
480 DATA193,201,200,144,1,96,173,90
490 DATA193,201,64,144,6,173,91,193
500 DATA240,1,96,173,92,193,141,96
510 DATA193,141,93,193,173,90,193,141
520 DATA97,193,141,94,193,173,91,193
530 DATA141,95,193,141,98,193,32,32
540 DATA192,96,1,2,4,8,16,32
550 DATA64,128
590 REM PLOT SINE CURVE
600 HIRES=49315:PLOT=49435
610 SYS(HIRES)
620 FOR I=0 TO 319
630 SYS(PLOT)(I,100+SIN(I/50)*80)
640 NEXT
650 GOTO 650
```

RASTER INTERRUPTS

The raster interrupt is one of the most powerful and versatile features of the Commodore 64. However, taking advantage of this feature requires some knowledge of machine language.

Raster interrupts take advantage of the sequential nature of the television display. The electron beam which draws the television image starts at the top left corner of the screen and traces horizontally accross the screen. When it reaches the right edge of the screen, it is turned off and brought back to the left side of the screen, at the same time being moved down a line. It repeats this process 312 times on a pal television (262 times on a NTSC set). At the bottom of the screen, the beam is turned off and returned to the upper left corner of the screen. Then the whole cycle is repeated again.

At any given time you can determine the line at which the beam is on by reading the raster register at location 53266 ($D012). This returns the lower 8 bits (0 — 255). The most significant bit is bit 7 of location 53265 ($D011). If this bit is set, add 255 to the previous value. The visible display area is located from line 51 to line 251.

When the raster register is written to (including the most significant bit),, the number that is written is saved for use with a raster compare function. When the actual raster value becomes the same as this number, bit 0 of the interrupt status register at location 53273 ($D019) is set to 1. If bit 0 of the interrupt enable register at location53274 ($D01A) has been set to 1 previously, an IRQ interrupt will occur.

When the Commodore 64 responds to an IRQ interrupt it saves all registers before jumping through the hardware IRQ interrupt vector at location 788 ($311) and 789 ($312). This is where the programmer can gain control of the interrupt process.

A new interrupt routine must be written and its address must be stored in locations 788 (low byte) and 789 (high byte). This routine should first check to see if the interrupt is indeed a raster interrupt and not the keyboard or timer A interrupt. If it is not a raster interrupt, control should be returned to the normal interrupt routine at location $EA31. However, if it is a raster interrupt then to turn subsequent raster interrupts on, a 1 must be written to bit 0 of the interrupt status register. Exit your interrupt routine by jumping to location $FEBC.

Helicopter demonstrates the entire process involved in setting up a raster interrupt. It is a simple program that puts 16 sprites on the screen by changing the vertical position of the sprites with a raster interrupt.
The applications to which raster interrupts can be put are quite diverse. As seen above, sprite registers can be changed, enabling the programmer to have up to 8 entirely different sprites on every vertical line if need be. Colour registers can be changed as can character sets. It is also possible to mix graphics modes. This is demonstrated in the

146

program SPLIT SCREEN. The top half of the screen is in normal text mode, while bottom half is bit mapped.

You may notice that the border between the 2 modes jumps around at times. This is because the raster interrupt is an IRQ interrupt and is therefore queued up after previous interrupts. This problem can be remedied by adding the following line which turns off keyboard interrupts.
1045 POKE 56334, PEEK (56334) AND 254

The afore-mentioned technique for handling raster interrupts may also be used to handle sprite-data collisions, sprite-sprite collisions and light pen negative transitions. Simply use the following table when writing to the interrupt enable register and reading the interrupt status register.

bit #	description
0	raster interrupt
1	sprite-data collision
2	sprite-sprite collision
3	lightpen negative transition

Note: Before attempting any cassette I/O the normal hardward IRQ vector **MUST** be restored.

HELICOPTER

```
10 PRINT"◌"
90 REM INTERRUPT CODE DATA
100 FOR I=0 TO 61:READ A:POKE 49152+I,A:NEXT I
105 REM SPRITE DATA
110 FOR I=0 TO 32:READ A:POKE 832+I,A:NEXT I
120 FOR I=33 TO 62:POKE 832+I,0:NEXT I
125 REM ALL SPRITES POINT TO LOCATION 13
130 FOR I=2040 TO 2047 :POKE I,13:NEXT I
135 REM SPRITE COLORS
140 FOR I=53287 TO 53294:POKE I,4:NEXT I
145 REM HORIZONTAL POSITIONS
150 FOR I=0 TO 14 STEP 2:POKE 53248+I,24+12*I
    :NEXT I
155 REM VERTICAL POSITIONS
160 FOR I=53249 TO 53263 STEP 2:POKE I,60:NEXT I
500 POKE 53269,255:REM ENABLE SPRITES
510 POKE 56333,127:REM TURN OFF INTERRUPTS
520 REM CHANGE IRQ INTERRUPT VECTOR
530 POKE 788,0:POKE 789,192
540 POKE 53265,PEEK(53265)AND127
550 REM FIRST INTERRUPT AT LINE 100
560 POKE 53266,100
```

```
570 REM ENABLE INTERRUPTS AND RASTER ONES
580 POKE 56333,129:POKE 53274,129
590 REM ANIMATE HELICOPTER
600 POKE 833,0:POKE 834,0
610 FOR I=0 TO 50:NEXT I
620 POKE 833,255:POKE 834,255
630 FOR I=0 TO 50:NEXT I
640 GOTO 600
900 REM RASTER INTERRUPT
1000 DATA 173,25,208,41,1,208,3,76
1005 DATA 49,234,141,25,208,173,18,208,48,34
1010 DATA 169,160,141,18,208,169,100,141
1015 DATA 1,208,141,3,208,141,5,208,141
1020 DATA 7,208,141,9,208,141,11,208
1025 DATA 141,13,208,141,15,208,76,188,254
1030 DATA 169,90,141,18,208,169,60,24
1035 DATA 144,219
2000 REM SPRITE DATA
2010 DATA 0,255,255,0,0,128,96,0
2015 DATA 123,144,1,240,159,255,200,103,255,254
2020 DATA 0,14,127,0,6,127,0,3
2030 DATA 254,0,0,32,0,15,255
```

The machine language source code for this program is included as a matter of interest for machine language programmers:

```
10 irqint        lda $d019
20 ;read interrupt status register
30               and #1
40 ;is it a raster interrupt?
50               bne i1
60 ;if not then jump to normal interrupt
     routine
70               jmp $ea31
80 ;reset raster interrupts
90 i1            sta $d019
100 ;current raster line
110              lda $d012
120 ;branch if greater than 128
130              bmi i3
140 ;next interrupt at line
150              lda #180
```

```
160              sta $d012
170 ;sprite vertical position
180              lda #100
190 ;sprite vertical registers
200 i2           sta $d001
210              sta $d003
220              sta $d005
230              sta $d007
240              sta $d009
250              sta $d00b
260              sta $d00d
270              sta $d00f
280 ;normal interrupt exit routine
290              jmp $febc
300 ;next raster at line 90
310 i3           lda #90
320              sta $d012
330 ;sprite vertical position
340              lda #80
350              clc
360 ;relative branch
370              bcc i2
```

SPLIT SCREEN

```
1000 REM READ IN INTERRUPT ROUTINE
1010 FOR I=0 TO 59:READ A:POKE 49152+I,A:NEXT
1020 POKE 56333,127:REM DISABLE INTERRUPTS
1030 POKE788,0:POKE789,192
1040 REM CHANGE IRQ INTERRUPT VECTOR
1050 POKE53265,PEEK(53265)AND127
1060 REM FIRST RASTER INTERRUPT AT LINE 30
1070 POKE 53266,30
1080 REM TURN INTERRUPTS ON
1090 POKE 56333,129:POKE53274,129
1100 POKE 53281,0:REM BACKGROUND COLOR
1110 BA=2*4096:REM BIT MAP BASE
1120 REM CLEAR BOTTOM HALF OF BIT MAP
1130 FORI=BA+3520TOBA+7999:POKEI,0:NEXT
1140 REM SET COLORS
1150 FOR I=1504 TO 2024:POKEI,16:NEXT
```

```
2000 FOR X=0TO319STEP.5:REM DRAW CURVE
2010 Y=ABS( INT( 90+80*ABS( SIN( X/10))))
2020 CH=INT( X/8)
2030 RO=INT( Y/8)
2040 LN=YAND7
2050 BY=BA+RO*320+8*CH+LN
2060 BI=7-( XAND7 )
2070 POKEBY,PEEK( BY)OR( 2↑BI )
2080 NEXT X
3000 PRINT"▥":LIST
5000 DATA173,25,208,41,1,208,3,76
5010 DATA49,234,141,25,208,173,18,208
5020 DATA48,21,173,17,208,41,95,141
5030 DATA17,208,169,21,141,24,208,169
5040 DATA145,141,18,208,76,188,254,173
5050 DATA17,208,9,32,141,17,208,169
5060 DATA25,141,24,208,169,30,141,18
5070 DATA208,76,188,254
```

The machine language source code for this program is included as a matter of interest for machine language programmers:

```
10 splitint     lda $d019
20 ;read interrupt status register
30              and #1
40              bne int1
50 ;if not raster interrupt go to normal routine
60              jmp $ea31
70 ;reset raster interrupts
80 int1         sta $d019
90 ;read raster register
100             lda $d012
110 ;branch if greater than 128
120             bmi int2
130 :turn off bit map
140             lda $d011
150             and #95
160             sta $d011
170 ;reset char base
180             lda #21
190             sta $d018
200 ;next interrupt
210             lda #145
```

```
220                  sta $d012
230 ;exit interrupt routine
240                  jmp $febc
250 ;turn on bit map
260 int2         lda $d011
270                  ora #32
280                  sta $d011
290 ;change char base
300                  lda #25
310                  sta $d018
320 ;next interrupt
330                  lda #30
340                  sta $d012
350 ;exit
360                  jmp $febc
```

CHAPTER 7

EXTERNAL DEVICES

The Commodore 64 system can be upgraded with the addition of external devices (peripherals). In this chapter we will describe the more common of these devices - the Datasette, floppy disk drives and printers.

DATASETTE

This is the most economical method of data storage. Its disadvantages, in comparison to disk drives, are that it is relatively slow and can only store program and data files sequentially. So, to access a file that has been passed on the tape, you must manually rewind it. It is a good idea to keep a record of the locations of programs with the tape counter so that they can be quickly located. For the same reason it is best to use short tapes. Even fast forward takes a lot of time to run through a 90 minute tape.

Unlike most microcomputer systems the Commodore 64 requires a particular cassette recorder, the Datasette. This has circuitry which enables the Commodore 64 to sense whether certain keys are pressed. It can therefore prompt the user when the required key is not pressed. Unfortunately it cannot discriminate between record and play modes. This means that it is still possible to inadvertently write over programs you had meant to read.

Write-protecting tapes

On the near edge of cassettes you will find two write-protect tabs, one for each side of the tape. Breaking these out will lock out the RECORD key, so you will be unable to write onto that side of the tape. Use this method to protect programs with which you do not want to run the risk of overwriting. You can reverse the write-protect by placing a piece of tape over the write-protect opening.

Care of tapes

Avoid touching the tape surface. The oils on your skin can destroy the oxide coating, thus corrupting your data. Store cassettes away from magnetic fields, which can also corrupt data. Television sets produce quite a strong magnetic field, so don't store tapes on or near them.
Relevant BASIC commands
SAVE, LOAD, GET#, INPUT#, OPEN, CLOSE

FLOPPY DISK DRIVES

The Commodore 64 can use any of the Commodore disk drives, but the model 1541 is designed to connect directly to the Commodore 64. Other models need an interface cartridge.

Disk drives are more flexible and provide faster access than the Datasette. They can store and access data randomly on any part of the diskette surface. Their disadvantage is that, being precise electromechanical devices, they are expensive.

Diskettes come in a protective jacket. Under no circumstances should the diskette be removed from this jacket.

Data storage on diskette

Each diskette used by the 1541 consists of 35 concentric circles called tracks. Each track is broken up into sectors, each of which holds 256 bytes.

Tracks 1-17 have 21 sectors/track
Tracks 18-24 have 19 sectors/track
Tracks 25-30 have 18 sectors/track
Tracks 31-35 have 17 sectors/track
Thus 1 1541 diskette can hold 174,848 bytes (170.75K)

Types of diskette

If you rotate the diskette within its jacket you will find one or more holes which align with the small hole in the jacket. If there is only one hole, the diskette is soft-sectored. If there is more than one hole, the diskette is hard-sectored. The 1541 drive uses only soft-sectored diskettes.

Loading and Unloading Diskettes

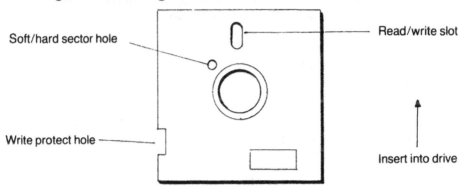

To load a diskette, gently slide it, in the orientation shown above, into the drive slot until it clicks in. Close the slot door. The drive will not operate with the door open.

To unload, press the slot door down and release. The door will open and the diskette will be ejected an inch or so. Remove it carefully.

There are two indicator lights on the drive. The green one is a power-on indicator. The red one lights only when there is some disk activity.

Formatting Diskettes

Before use, a new diskette must be formatted. This writes a disk name, ID number and track and sector information onto the diskette. Formatting is done by the commands:

```
OPEN 1, 8, 15
PRINT#1, "NEW : diskname, ID"
```
The diskname can be any string up to 16 characters long. The ID number should be different for every diskette.

A shorter version of the format command used on diskettes which have previously been formatted will erase all data on the diskette and rename it, leaving the ID number unchanged.
```
OPEN 1, 8, 15
PRINT#1, "NEW : diskname"
```
Note: NEW may be abbreviated to N

Block Availability Map (BAM) and Initialization

The BAM is found on track 18. It contains memory allocation information used when the disk drive is accessed. Each time this happens, the drive compares the ID number on the diskette with the ID number held in drive memory. If they don't match, the drive loads the diskette BAM into drive memory and uses this copy to access the diskette. This copying is called initialization. If the ID numbers match, initialization is not carried out. This is why different diskettes should be given different ID numbers. If they're not, the situation could arise where the BAM for another diskette with the same ID number is used to access a diskette. At best this will cause searches to be unsuccessful. At worst programs will be overwritten.

However, if you have given diskettes the same ID numbers, you can force the drive to copy the BAM using the following:
```
OPEN 1,8,15
PRINT#1 "INITIALIZE"
```
This can be abbreviated to:
```
OPEN 1,8,15,"I"
```

Diskette Directory

This is located on track 18. It contains the names, starting sector addresses and file types of all files on the diskette. It can be displayed using the following commands
```
LOAD "$",8
LIST
```

Write-protecting Diskettes

Like cassette tapes, diskettes can be write-protected. This is done by covering the write-protect slot on the edge of the diskette jacket with tape. Removing the tape restores the diskette to read/write condition.

File Manipulation Commands

Renaming files.
This is done with the commands:
```
OPEN 1,8,15
PRINT#1,"RENAME : NEW—NAME=OLD—NAME"
```
R is an acceptable abbreviation for RENAME

Erasing files
This is done with the commands:
>   OPEN 1,8,15
>   PRINT# 1, "SCRATCH : FILENAME"
>   S is an acceptable abbreviation for SCRATCH

Copying files
This is done with the commands:
>   OPEN 1,8,15
>   PRINT# 1,"COPY : NEW—NAME = OLD–NAME"
>   C is an acceptable abbreviation for COPY

Joining files
This is done with the commands:
>   OPEN 1,8,15
>   PRINT# 1,"COPY : NEW—FILE=FILE1,FILE2

Note: Disk command strings must not be greater than 40 characters in length.

VALIDATE
This command does housekeeping on the diskette, deleting any files that were not properly closed, and freeing blocks which may have been allocated as temporary storage but are not now associated with any file.

Multiple Disk Systems

If you have a multiple disk system you may need to assign different device numbers to the different drives. At power-up they are all device number 8. Drives can have device numbers 8, 9, 10 and 11. To change the device number:

1) Turn off all drives but the one you are changing
2) Open a command file to the device
   e.g. OPEN 1, 8, 15
3) Type PRINT# 1, "M-W" CHR$ (119) CHR$ (0) CHR$ (2) CHR$ (new-device-number + 32) CHR$ (new-device-number + 64)

Leave that drive on. Turning it off will erase the new device number. Turn on the next drive you want to change. This is now device 8 so you already have a command channel open to it. If you want to change it or have more drives be sure to use a different device number.

Closing Disk Files

When a program writes to, or reads from, a disk, the data is first placed in a buffer. Only when the buffer is full is the data actually written to the diskette or, only when it is empty is more data read in. Thus, if you finish writing to the disk with the buffer not full, this data will not be stored on disk. To avoid this, you must close the file. This automatically writes the buffered data to disk, whether or not the buffer is full.

Maximum Number of Opened Files

The Commodore 64 can only handle 10 open files at a time, and only 5 of these to disk. It is therefore a good idea to close all files immediately after use.

Disk Data Files

Three types of file can be stored on disk. Program files have already been dealt with. The other two are sequential and random access files.

Sequential Files
These must first be opened using the following format:
OPEN lf , dev , sa , "dn : filename , SEQ , W"

lf	-	logical file number
dev	-	device number
sa	-	secondary address
dn	-	drive number - this may be omitted on single-drive systems
SEQ	-	indicates sequential file
W	-	indicates write mode - it can also be R for read.

e.g. OPEN 1, 8, 4, "0 : RECIPES , SEQ , W"
To overwrite an existing file use an "@" before the drive number.
e.g. OPEN 1, 8, 4, "@0 : RECIPES , SEQ , W"
This also applies to program files.
e.g. SAVE "@0 : PROG-NAME" , 8

Random Access files
These are created by directly addressing diskette sectors and memory buffers. There are 8 buffers available on the Commodore 64 but 4 of these are used by the BAM, variable space, command channel I/O and the disk controller, so don't open more than 4 buffers at a time. The format for opening a random access file is as follows:
       OPEN lf,dev,sa,"#buff nr"

lf	-	logical file number: 2-14 for data transfer, 15 for utility commands (see below)
dev	-	device number
sa	-	secondary address (2-14)
buff nr	-	buffer number. This can be ommitted as the Disk Operating System (DOS) will automatically select one.

Information is written to random access files using the PRINT# command

Disk Utility Instructions

Block-Read

Purpose	-	reads any sector into one of the memory buffers
To use	-	1) Open a command channel
		OPEN 15,8,15
		2) Open a direct access channel
		e.g. OPEN 2,8,4,"#"

3) Specify track and sector and read it in.

PRINT#15,"B-R:"sa;dn;T;S

sa - secondary address from 2 above

dn - drive number - mandatory when using direct access commands

You may now use GET# and INPUT# to get the data from the buffer.

e.g. GET#2,B

Check ST for end of data

Close all files when you are through.

Note: B-R is an acceptable abbreviation for BLOCK-READ

BLOCK-ALLOCATE

Purpose - checks a sector to see whether it is availabe or already allocated. If available it marks it in the BAM as allocated. If already allocated, it leaves the BAM unchanged and returns the next available track and sector in the error channel. If no sector is available it returns track 0, sector 0, which is non-existent. If the sector you initially asked for is available the message 'OK' is returned in the error channel.

To use - 1) Open command channel

OPEN 15,8,15

2) Specify track and sector and check it.

PRINT#15,"B-A":0;T;S

T - Track number

S - Sector number

3) Check error channel

INPUT#15,E,EM$,T,S

E - error code

EM$ - error message

T - track

S - sector

Proceed on the basis of the error channel return.

4) Close channels

Note: B-A is an acceptable abbreviation for BLOCK-ALLOCATE

BLOCK-WRITE

Purpose - To write data to a sector specified by you. With this instruction you can write to the BAM or the directory, thus destroying them, so it is wise ro use a BLOCK-ALLOCATE first, to find a free sector.

To use - 1) Do a BLOCK-ALLOCATE (not mandatory, but wise)

2) If EM$='OK' or other free sector returned, continue

3) Open direct access file

e.g. OPEN3,8,4,"#"

4) PRINT# the data - from DATA statements, arrays keyboard

e.g. PRINT#3,A

5) The data is now in the buffer. To block-write it use:

PRINT#15,"B-W:"4;0;T;S

6) Close files

Note: 1) The format for the BLOCK—WRITE instruction is the same as for BLOCK-READ

2) B—W is an acceptable abbreviation for BLOCK-READ

BUFFER-POINTER

Purpose   - To change the buffer pointer to start GETting at a particular byte, rather than starting at the first byte in the buffer

To use   - 1) Do a block-read to the point where you are about to GET# bytes

2) Change the buffer pointer

e.g. PRINT#15,"B-P:"sa;byte

sa - secondary address used in setting up the direct access file

byte - number of byte you want to start GETting at

e.g. PRINT#15,"B-P:"4;47

Note: B-P is an acceptable abbreviation for BUFFER-POINTER

BLOCK-FREE

Purpose   - to de-allocate any block on the disk.

To use   - 1) Open command channel

OPEN15,8,15

2) Specify track and sector and free it

PRINT#15,"B-F:"dr;T;S

dr - drive number

T - track number

S - sector number

e.g. PRINT#15,"B-F:"0;1;4

Note: B-F is an acceptable abbreviation for BLOCK-FREE

Disk Drive Memory Manipulation

The 1541 drive controller contains a 6502 microprocessor. It has 2K of RAM and DOS, which resides on ROM. Some of the RAM is used for housekeeping. The rest is used for buffers. This is also available to the programmer for machine code programs.

The buffers are:

Buffer	Address (hex)
1	300 - 3FF
2	400 - 4FF
3	500 - 5FF

4	600 - 6FF
5	700 - 7FF

Buffer 5 is often used by DOS, so it is not advisable to use it for machine language programs. If you intend to use buffer space for machine code, specify the buffers you want for direct access files, rather than leaving it up to DOS which may overwrite your machine code if left to its own devices.

MEMORY-WRITE

Purpose	-	to store machine code in drive memory
To use	-	a singe M-W commands allows you to store up to 34 bytes
	-	All the data must be transferred as character strings using CHR$
	-	The number of bytes to be stored must be indicated
	-	ONLY the abbreviation M—W can be used. MEMORY—WRITE, in full, is unacceptable
	-	The machine code must end with an RTS instruction. Otherwise the 1541 may loop endlessly, or do something catastrophic to the data on the diskette.

1) Open command channel and transfer data
   OPEN 15, 8, 15
   PRINT# 15, "M-W" CHR$ (LO-ADDRESS-BYTE) CHR$ (HI-ADDRESS-BYTE) CHR$ (NR-BYTES-TRANSFERRED) CHR$ (BYTE-1) CHR$ (BYTE-2)...
   CLOSE 15

MEMORY-READ

Purpose	-	to read data from drive memory one byte at a time

To use:	-	The byte read is transferred through the error channel so use GET # 15 to get it
	-	ONLY the abbreviation M-R is acceptable. MEMORY-READ, in full, is not
	-	The address to be read is specified using CHR$, as for MEMORY-WRITE

1) Open command channel
   OPEN 15,8,15
2) Specify address and read
   PRINT#15, "M-R"CHR$(LO-ADDRESS-BYTE) CHR$(HI-ADDRESS-BYTE)
   GET#15,A$
   PRINTA$
   CLOSE 15

MEMORY-EXECUTE

Purpose	-	to run a machine language program loaded into drive memory by MEMORY-WRITE
To use	-	ONLY the abbreviation M-E is acceptable

1) Open command channel
OPEN 15,8,15
2) Specify start address of routine and execute
PRINT#15,"M-E"CHR$(LO-ADDRESS-BYTE)CHR$(HI-ADDRESS-BYTE)
3) Close channel
CLOSE 15

User Commands

U1

Purpose	-	similar to B-R. The only difference is that U1 reads the 2 bytes preceding the data in the sector. These bytes are the link address to the next sector in the file, giving track and sector.
To use	-	same as B-R, but replace B-R with U1.

U2

Purpose	-	similar to B-W. The difference is that B-W terminates the file at the sector written. U2 allows you to write the link address, ie. track and sector - to the next sector in the file
To use	-	same as B-W but replace B-W with U2

U3-U9

Purpose	-	similar to M-E but they cause a jump to specific locations as given below:

U3	$0500
U4	$0503
U5	$0506
U6	$0509
U7	$050C
U8	$050F
U9	$FFFA

These locations are only 3 bytes long as they are intended to hold a JMP instruction to a location the programmer defines.

U (or UJ)

Purpose	-	jumps to DOS to its power-up routine
To use	-	all the U3-J commands have the following syntax for use:

OPEN 15,8,15
PRINT#15,"U4"
CLOSE15

160

The 1515 Graphic Printer

This has a built in character set including upper and lower case letters, numbers and graphics. To access the printer you must first open a file to it using the following syntax:

OPEN lf,dev,sa

lf   -   logical file number (0-255)

dev   -   device number - either 4 or 5 - it is selected using a switch at the rear of the printer

sa   -   used to select between character sets. If omitted the default character set (upper case & graphics) is used.
         If sa = 7 the alternate character set (lower case) is selected.

Having opened a channel to the printer you now use PRINT# lf to print your data.

Print Formatting

Comma

If the PRINT# data items are seperated by a comma the print puts 11 spaces between items printed.

Semicolon

This has the same effect as it does on a screen display

TAB and SPC

These cannot appear immediately after a PRINT#
ie. PRINT#1,TAB(6) is illegal; PRINT#1,"";TAB(6) is OK
On the printer, both TAB and SPC have the same effect as SPC does on the screen display

POS

This reproduces the screen TAB function on the printer. That is, it starts printing at an absolute position rather than relative to where the current printing is being done.

POS is sent to the printer as CHR$(16). The two characters immediately following this determine the print position.

e.g.   PRINT#1,CHR(16);"16";"starts printing at column 16"

Printer Graphics

The printer has several modes, in which characters received are treated differently. The modes and commands to get into them are shown below:

Mode	Command
Double-width characters	CHR$ (14)
Single-width characters	CHR$ (15)
Reverse characters	CHR$ (18) or "[CTRL] [RVS ON]"
Normal characters	CHR$ (146) or "[CTRL] [RVS OFF]"
Graphics	CHR$ (8)
Alternate character set	CHR$ (17)
Standard character set	CHR$ (143)
Repeat Graphics	CHR$ (26)

These are used in PRINT# statements

e.g.   PRINT#1,CHR$(17);"LOWER CASE"

Apart from the following two, the functions of the modes are obvious

GRAPHICS mode

This is similar to defining custom character sets in character memory in that it creates patterns of dots. However, in printer graphics, rows not columns are given values, as below, and columns, not rows, are added.

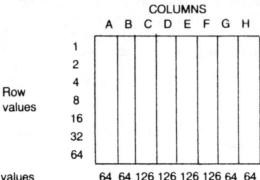

Note that only 7 rows are used.

To print this character do the following:

　　　OPEN# 1 , 4 - open a channel to the printer

　　　PRINT# 1 , CHR$ (8) - get into graphics mode

　　　PRINT# 1 , CHR$ (64 + 128) ; CHR$ (64 + 128) ; CHR$ (126 + 128) ; CHR$ (126 + 128) ; CHR$ (126 + 128) ; CHR$ (126 + 128) ; CHR$ (64 + 128) ; CHR$ (64 + 128)

Note that the column values are added to 128. It would of course have been simpler to put the column values in a DATA statement and read and PRINT#ed them in a loop.

Repeat Graphics Mode

This mode allows you to repeat a pattern of seven vertical dots up to 255 times per command.

e.g.   OPEN 1,4 - open a channel to the printer

　　　PRINT# 1 , CHR$ (26) CHR$ (5) CHR$ (255)

the first CHR$ value puts the printer into repeat graphics mode. The second CHR$ value sets the number of repeat(s). The third CHR$ value defines the vertical dot pattern (in this case just a solid bar 7 dots high)

These two lines will just cause 5 bars to be printed. There is no space between them, they're continuous.

Games Controls

There are three types of games controls in common use - the keyboard, joysticks and paddles. This section describes these, and how they are used.

Keyboard

This is the most common device for games control. Keys are assigned to various functions, such as move left, move right, fire, etc.

When choosing keys for your games, ensure that they are easily usable. Their position should reflect their function. For example, if you have 4 keys for up, down, left and right, use keys in corresponding positions, as below:

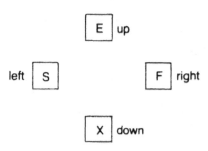

The space bar makes a good fire button since it's large and hard to miss. It is annoying to have to repeatedly press and release keys to repeat an action, so you should set all keys so that they automatically repeat when held down. This is done by POKEing 128 into byte 650. POKEing 0 into this byte makes only the cursor control keys repeat automatically.

Checking the keyboard.

GET is the command to use to check the keyboard, as it doesn't echo the character typed in, or stop the program to wait for input. It merely checks the keyboard buffer and continues. If there is no character in the buffer the GET variable is set to 0 or the null string. If there is a character in the buffer it is assigned to the variable and the buffer is cleared. The GET variable should be a string variable, since this will accept almost any keystroke (except STOP, RESTORE, SHIFT, CTRL, ◀ and the colour control keys). If a numeric variable is used you will only be able to GET numeric characters without causing an error.

Having got the character, the program must decide what to do. This can be done in various ways.
(i)   Repeated IF-THEN-
e.g.   10 GET K$
         20 IF K$ = "S" THEN - : GOTO 70
         30 IF K$ = "E" THEN - : GOTO 70
         40 IF K$ = "X" THEN - : GOTO 70
         50 IF K$ = "F" THEN - : GOTO 70
         60 IF K$ = " " THEN - : GOTO 70
         70

163

The statements after the THEN may carry out the required actions and then branch past the rest of the IF statements. If the actions required are too complex to fit on a line, the program may GOTO or GOSUB a section of code to carry out the actions.

(ii)   ON-GOTO-

If you are using many keys, going through all the IF statements may be too time-consuming. It may be quicker to use some calculation or ASCII values with an ON statement. The disadvantage of this technique is that the ASCII values of the characters you are using may be widely seperated, necessitating complex calculations which take as much time as stepping through the IF statements.

Joystick

This consists of a moveable stick and a fire button. When moved, the stick closes 1 or 2 of 4 switches.

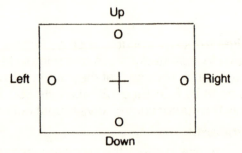

If the stick is moved upor down or to one side, only one switch is closed. If it is moved diagonally, the two switches it moves between are closed.

The state of the switches can be discovered by PEEKing certain memory locations. Each switch controls one bit, delivering a 0 when the switch is closed, a 1 when the switch is open.

7	6	5	4	3	2	1	0
			FIRE	RIGHT	LEFT	DOWN	UP

(Bits used by location 56320 and 56321 for joystick ports 1 and 2 respectively)

Since the program must check individual bits, bit masks must be used. For example, to check the fire button bit — only use:

FB = PEEK (56320) AND 16

If FB = 0 then the Fire button has been pushed.

The joystick direction is checked by using the following statement:

$$DIR = 15—(PEEK (56320) \text{ AND } 15)$$

The direction is determined by the following table:

DIR	Direction
0	None
1	Up
2	Down
3	—
4	Left
5	Up and Left
6	Down and Left
7	—
8	Right
9	Up and Right
10	Down and Right

The following program demonstrates joystick control:

```
10 REM * JOY STICK DEMO *
20 FOR P=0 TO 10
30 READ X,Y
40 X$(P)=CHR$(X) : Y$(P)=CHR$(Y)
50 NEXT P
60 DATA 0,0,0,145,0,17,0,0,157,0,157,145,157,
17,0,0,29,0,29,145,29,17
100 JOY=56320 :PRINT CHR$(147)
110 PRINT"X";CHR$(157);
120 IF (PEEK(JOY)AND16)=0 THEN PRINT"●";
CHR$(157);
130 P=15-(PEEK(JOY)AND15)
140 PRINT " ";CHR$(157);X$(P);Y$(P);
150 GOTO 110
```

Paddles

Paddles are used in place of joysticks where a variable control of direction is needed (e.g. moving a racquet up and down the screen for tennis, etc.). Each port can take two paddles, one for the x-direction and one for the y-direction.

The paddles are read into memory locations 54297 and 54298. These are the sound chip's paddle read registers.

A paddle set to zero position and rotated through to its maximum rotation will return values from 0 to 255 in increments of 1. Owing to such a large

165

range of possible output values and the rate that they can change, it is impossible for BASIC to keep up with the paddles.

However, the 'REGLINK' routine used in the Sound chapter can be modified to link the output of the paddles to the x and y co-ordinates of a Sprite. Use the following method to link Sprite#0 to the paddles.

1. Connect paddles to port labelled 'Port-2'
2. Load 'REGLINK' (listed on page 67) and change Line 110 to:
      110 DATA 208
3. RUN "REGLINK" with the above change
4. LOAD "SQUARE" from Graphics chapter (listed on page 94)
5. Type: POKE 820, 0 : POKE 821, 1
6. RUN Square

You should be able to move the Sprite square around the screen independently of the operating system.

Appendix A

1) CHR$ Value Codes

Character	CHR$ Code	Character	CHR$ Code
	0	#	35
	1	$	36
	2	%	37
STOP	3	&	38
	4	'	39
WHITE	5	(	40
	6	)	41
	7	*	42
	8	+	43
	9	,	44
	10	—	45
	11	.	46
	12	/	47
RETURN	13	0	48
Lower case switch	14	1	49
	15	2	50
	16	3	51
CRSR ↓	17	4	52
RVS ON	18	5	53
CLR/HOME	19	6	54
INST/DEL	20	7	55
	21	8	56
	22	9	57
	23	:	58
	24	;	59
	25	<	60
	26	=	61
	27	>	62
RED	28	?	63
CSRS →	29	@	64
GREEN	30	A	65
BLUE	31	B	66
space	32	C	67
!	33	D	68
"	34	E	69

Character	CHR$ Code	Character	CHR$ Code
F	70	◨	109
G	71	▨	110
H	72	▢	111
I	73	▢	112
J	74	▣	113
K	75	▤	114
L	76	♥	115
M	77	▨	116
N	78	▧	117
O	79	⊠	118
P	80	▣	119
Q	81	♣	120
R	82	▨	121
S	83	♦	122
T	84	⊞	123
U	85	▥	124
V	86	▨	125
W	87	π	126
X	88	�	127
Y	89		128
Z	90		129
[	91		130
£	92	SHIFT RUN/STOP.	131
]	93		132
↑	94	f1	133
←	95	f3	134
▤	96	f5	135
♠	97	f7	136
▨	98	f2	137
▨	99	f4	138
▨	100	f6	139
▨	101	f8	140
▨	102	SHIFT RETURN	141
▨	103	Upper case switch	142
▨	104		143
▨	105	BLACK	144
▨	106	CRSR ↑	145
▨	107	RVS OFF	146
▢	108	CLR/HOME	147

168

Character	CHR$ Code	Character	CHR$ Code
INST/DEL	148	▯	170
	149	▯	171
	150	▯	172
	151	▯	173
	152	▯	174
	153	▭	175
	154	▯	176
	155	▯	177
PURPLE	156	▤	178
CRSR ←	157	▯	179
YELLOW	158	▯	180
CYAN	159	▯	181
space	160	▯	182
▯	161	▯	183
▭	162	▯	184
▭	163	▭	185
▯	164	▯	186
▯	165	▯	187
▨	166	▯	188
▯	167	▯	189
▨	168	▯	190
◪	169	▨	191

Codes 192-223 are the same as 96-127
Codes 224-254 are the same as 160-190
Code 255 is the same as code 126

---

2) Screen Codes

Character Set 1	Character Set 2	Screen Code
ə		0
A	a	1
B	b	2
C	c	3
D	d	4
E	e	5
F	f	6
G	g	7

Character Set 1	Character Set 2	Screen Code
H	h	8
I	i	9
J	j	10
K	k	11
L	l	12
M	m	13
N	n	14
O	o	15
P	p	16
Q	q	17
R	r	18
S	s	19
T	t	20
U	u	21
V	v	22
W	w	23
X	x	24
Y	y	25
Z	z	26
[		27
£		28
]		29
↑		30
←		31
space		32
!		33
"		34
#		35
$		36
%		37
&		38
'		39
(		40
)		41
*		42
+		43
,		44
−		45
.		46
/		47

Character Set 1	Character Set 2	Screen Code
0		48
1		49
2		50
3		51
4		52
5		53
6		54
7		55
8		56
9		57
:		58
;		59
<		60
=		61
>		62
?		63
⊡		64
♠	A	65
⊟	B	66
⊡	C	67
⊡	D	68
⊡	E	69
⊡	F	70
⊡	G	71
⊡	H	72
◰	I	73
◰	J	74
◪	K	75
☐	L	76
◩	M	77
◪	N	78
☐	O	79
☐	P	80
◼	Q	81
⊔	R	82
♥	S	83
⊡	T	84
◪	U	85
⊠	V	86

Character Set 1	Character Set 2	Screen Code
⧉	W	87
✛	X	88
⊡	Y	89
◆	Z	90
⊞		91
▣		92
⊡		93
π	❅	94
◣	░	95
space		96
◧		97
▬		98
▢		99
▢		100
▢		101
▓		102
▢		103
▭		104
◢	░	105
◪		106
⊞		107
◪		108
◩		109
◲		110
▢		111
◰		112
⊟		113
⊞		114
▤		115
▢		116
◧		117
▢		118
▢		119
▢		120
▢		121
▢		122
◪		123
◱		124
◪		125

172

Character Set 1	Character Set 2	Screen Code
◪		126
◪		127

Codes 128-255 produce reversed images of codes 0-127

---

3) ASCII Codes

Character	Code	Character	Code
NULL	0	GS	29
SOH	1	RS	30
STX	2	US	31
ETX	3	space	32
EOT	4	!	33
ENQ	5	"	34
ACK	6	#	35
BEL	7	$	36
BS	8	%	37
HT	9	&	38
LF	10	'	39
VT	11	(	40
FF	12	)	41
CR	13	*	42
SO	14	+	43
SI	15	,	44
DLE	16	-	45
DC1	17	.	46
DC2	18	/	47
DC3	19	0	48
DC4	20	1	49
NAK	21	2	50
SYN	22	3	51
ETB	23	4	52
CAN	24	5	53
EM	25	6	54
SUB	26	7	55
ESC	27	8	56
FS	28	9	57

Character	Code	Character	Code
:	58	a	97
;	59	b	98
<	60	c	99
=	61	d	100
>	62	e	101
?	63	f	102
@	64	g	103
A	65	h	104
B	66	i	105
C	67	j	106
D	68	k	107
E	69	l	108
F	70	m	109
G	71	n	110
H	72	o	111
I	73	p	112
J	74	q	113
K	75	r	114
L	76	s	115
M	77	t	116
N	78	u	117
O	79	v	118
P	80	w	119
Q	81	x	120
R	82	y	121
S	83	z	122
T	84	;	123
U	85	<	124
V	86	=	125
W	87	>	126
X	88	DEL	127
Y	89		
Z	90		
[	91		
\	92		
]	93		
↑	94		
←	95		
space	96		

Appendix B

Complete Memory Map

Address (Decimal)	Description
0	Chip directional register
1 - 2	Memory and tape control
3 - 4	Floating point - fixed point vector
5 - 6	Fixed point - floating point vector
7	BASIC counter. Search character ':' or end of line
8	Scan-quotes flag
9	Column position of cursor on line
10	Flag ; 0 = LOAD, 1 = VERIFY
11	BASIC input buffer pointer ; subscript number
12	Default DIM flag
13	Variable type flag : FF = string, 00 = numeric
14	Numeric type flag : 80 = integer, 00 = floating point
15	DATA scan flag : LIST quote flag ; memory flag
16	Subscript flag ; FNx flag
17	Flag ; 0 = INPUT, 152 = READ, 64 = GET
18	ATN sign flag ; comparison evaluation flag
19	Current I/O prompt flag
20 - 21	Where BASIC stores integers used in calculations
22	Temporary string stack pointer
23 - 24	Last temporary string vector
25 - 33	Stack for temporary string descriptors
34 - 37	Utility pointer area
38 - 42	Product area for multiplication
43 - 44	Pointer to start of BASIC program
45 - 46	Pointer to end of BASIC program ; start of BASIC variables
47 - 48	Pointer to end of variables ; start of arrays
51 - 52	Pointer to start of string storage - strings move down from top of available memory towards arrays.
53 - 54	Pointer to end of string storage
55 - 56	Pointer to top of RAM available to BASIC
57 - 58	Current BASIC line number
59 - 60	Previous BASIC line number
61 - 62	Pointer to BASIC statement (for CONT)
63 - 64	Current DATA line number
65 - 66	Pointer to current DATA item
67 - 68	Jump vector for INPUT statement
69 - 70	Current variable name

71 - 72	Current variable address
73 - 74	Variable pointer for FOR/NEXT statement
75 - 76	Y save ; operator save ; BASIC pointer save
77	Comparison symbol
78 - 79	Work area ; function definition pointer
80 - 81	Work area ; string descriptor pointer
82	Length of string
83	Garbage collect use
84 - 86	Jump vector for functions
87 - 96	Numeric work area
97 - 102	Floating point accumulator 1 ; Exponent, 4 byte Mantissa, Sign
103	Series evaluation constant pointer
104	Accumulator 1 overflow
105 - 110	Floating point accumulator 2
111	Sign comparison - Acc 1 with Acc 2
112	Acc 2 rounding
113 - 114	Cassette buffer length ; series pointer
115 - 138	CHRGOT BASIC subroutine - gets next BASIC character
139 - 143	RND storage and work area
144	ST - status byte
145	STOP and REVERSE flags ; Keyswitch PIA
146	Timing constant for tape
147	Flag : 0 = LOAD, 1 = VERIFY
148	Serial output ; deferred character flag
150	Tape EOT received
151	Register save
152	Number of OPEN files
153	Current input device
154	Current output (CMD) device
155	Tape character parity
156	Flag : byte received
157	Output control flag : direct = 128 ; run = 0
158	Tape pass 1 error log
159	Tape pass 2 error log
160 - 162	Jifie clock - TI and TI$ use this
163	Serial bit count
164	Cycle count
165	Tape write bit count
166	Pointer to tape buffer
167	Tape write count ; input bit storage
168	Tape write new byte ; Read error ; input bit count
169	Write start bit ; Read bit error
170	Tape scan ; count
171	Write read length ; Read checksum ; parity

172 - 173	Pointer to tape buffer ; scrolling
174 - 175	Tape end addresses ; end of program
176 - 177	Tape timing constants
178 - 179	Pointer to start of tape buffer
180	Tape timer ; bit count
181	RS232 next bit to send
182	Read character error ; next byte out
183	Number of characters in current file name
184	Current logical file number
185	Current secondary address
186	Current device number
187 - 188	Pointer to current file name
189	Write shift byte ; Read input character
190	Number of blocks remaining to Read/Write
191	Serial word buffer
192	Tape motor interlock
193 - 194	I/O start addresses
195 - 196	KERNAL setup pointer
197	Current key pressed (see Appendix H)
198	Keyboard buffer counter
199	Flag : screen reverse - 1 is on, 0 is off
200	Pointer to end-of-line for input
201 - 202	Cursor log (row, column)
203	Current key pressed
204	Flag : cursor blink enable (0 is on)
205	Cursor blink delay
206	Character under cursor
207	Flag : cursor on/off
208	Input from screen/keyboard
209 - 210	Pointer to screen line on which cursor appears
211	Position of cursor on line
212	0 = direct cursor, else programmed
213	Screen line length, 21, 43, 65, 87
214	Current screen line number - To change cursor position, 201, 210, 211 and 214 must be changed
215	ASCII value of last character printed
216	Number of INSERTs outstanding
217 - 240	Screen line link table
241	Dummy screen line link
242	Screen row marker
243 - 244	Pointer to current location in colour memory
245 - 246	Pointer to keyscan table
247 - 248	Pointer to RS-232 receiver buffer start
249 - 250	Pointer to RS-232 transmitter buffer start
251 - 254	Free zero-page locations
255	BASIC storage

256 - 266	Float - ASCII work area
256 - 318	Tape error log
256 - 511	Processor stack area
512 - 600	BASIC input buffer
601 - 610	Logical file table for OPEN files
611 - 620	Device number table for OPEN files
621 - 630	Secondary address table
631 - 640	Keyboard buffer
641 - 642	Pointer to start of memory for operating system
643 - 644	Pointer to end of memory for operating system
645	Serial bus timeout flag
646	Current colour code (for PRINTed character)
647	Colour under cursor
648	Screen memory page indicator
649	Maximum length of keyboard buffer - must be less than 11
650	Key autorepeat (0 = cursor controls, 255 = all)
651	Pre-repeat delay
652	Inter-repeat delay
653	Keyboard flag for SHIFT, CTRL and C= keys. If SHIFT pressed, bit 0 is set, if CTRL, bit 1, if C=, bit 2
654	Last shift pattern
655 - 656	Pointer for keyboard table set-up
657	Shift mode (0 = enabled, 128 = disabled)
658	Auto scroll down flag (0 = on, else off)
659	RS-232 control register
660	RS-232 command register
661 - 662	Non-standard (bit time/2 -100)
663	RS-232 status register
664	Number of bits to send
665 - 666	Baud rate (full) bit time
667	Pointer to RS-232 receiver buffer (end)
668	Pointer to RS-232 receiver buffer (start)
669	Pointer to RS-232 transmit buffer (start)
670	Pointer to RS-232 transmit buffer (end)
671 - 672	Holds IRQ during tape operations
673	CIA 2 (NMI) Interrupt control
674	CIA 1 Timer A control log
675	CIA 1 Interrupt log
676	CIA 1 Timer A enable flag
677	Screen row marker
678	PAL/NISC flag, 0 = NTSC, 1 = PAL
679 - 767	UNUSED
768 - 769	Error message link
770 - 771	Basic warm start link

772 - 773	Tokenization routine link
774 - 775	Print tokens link
776 - 777	Start new BASIC code link
778 - 779	Get arithmetic element link
780	Temporary storage of A during SYS
781	Temporary storage of X during SYS
782	Temporary storage of Y during SYS
783	Temporary storage of P during SYS
784 - 785	USR function jump
788 - 789	Hardware interrupt vector (EA31)
790 - 791	Break (BRK) interrupt vector (FE66)
792 - 793	NMI interrupt vector (FE47)
794 - 795	OPEN vector (F34A)
796 - 797	CLOSE vector (F291)
798 - 799	Set input device vector (F20E)
800 - 801	Set output device vector (F250)
802 - 803	Restore I/O vector (F333)
804 - 805	Input vector (F157)
806 - 807	Output vector (F1CA)
808 - 809	Test STOP-key vector (F6ED)
810 - 811	GET vector (F13E)
812 - 813	Close all files vector (F32F)
814 - 815	User vector (FE66)
816 - 817	Load-from-device vector (F4A5)
818 - 819	Save to device vector (F5ED)
828 - 1019	Cassette buffer - useful for holding machine code when no files are being used
1024 - 2039	Screen memory
2040 - 2047	Sprite pointers
2048 - 40959	Basic programs and variables
32768 - 40959	ROM plug-in area
40960 - 49151	ROM Basic
49152 - 53247	Unused
53248 - 53294	6566 video chip
53248 - 57343	Character set
54272 - 54300	6581 Sound chip
55296 - 56319	Colour memory
56320 - 56335	6526 Interface chip-1
56576 - 56591	6526 Interface chip-2
57344 - 65535	ROM operating system
57344 - 65535	Unused
65409 - 65525	Jump table including the following:
65478	Set Input channel
65481	Set Output channel
65484	Restore default I/O channels
65487	INPUT

65490	PRINT
65505	Test STOP key
65508	GET

Appendix C

Keyboard Graphics and how to get them.

Symbol	Keypress	Symbol	Keypress
	⊄ E **		⊄ R
	⊄ W		⊄ Q
	⊄ D		⊄ F
	⊄ C		⊄ V
	⊄ B		⊄ +
	⊄ T		⊄ Y
	⊄ U		⊄ I
	⊄ O		⊄ P
	⊄ ∂		⊄ −
	⊄ 8		⊄ H
	⊄ J		⊄ K
	⊄ L		⊄ N
	⊄ M		⊄ £
	⊄ S		⊄ X
	⊄ A		⊄ Z
	⊄ *		
	SHIFT L		SHIFT ∂
	SHIFT O		SHIFT P
	SHIFT I		SHIFT U
	SHIFT K		SHIFT J
	SHIFT W		SHIFT Q
	SHIFT +		SHIFT V
	SHIFT M		SHIFT N
◆	SHIFT Z	♥	SHIFT S
✚	SHIFT X	♠	SHIFT A
	SHIFT E		SHIFT D
	SHIFT *		SHIFT C
	SHIFT F		SHIFT R
	SHIFT T		SHIFT G
	SHIFT B		SHIFT −
	SHIFT H		SHIFT Y
	SHIFT £		
↑	UP ARROW	←	LEFT ARROW
π	PI		

As well as these there are a set of symbols
used to represent control characters such as color
controls and cursor controls.

The symbols vary depending upon whether the
computer is in upper case or lower case mode.

The symbols are:

Upper case.

Symbol	Keypress
♥	CLR
▨	HOME
▨	cursor down
▢	cursor up
▶	cursor right
▌▌	cursor left
▄	ctrl 1
▣	ctrl 2
▨	ctrl 3
▲	ctrl 4
▆	ctrl 5
▥	ctrl 6
▨	ctrl 7
▥	ctrl 8
▨	ctrl 9
▆	ctrl 0

Lower case

Symbol	Keypress
▣	HOME
▨	cursor down
▨	ctrl 2
▨	ctrl 4
▨	ctrl 8
▨	ctrl 9

‡‡ The ⊂ symbol is the special shift key
located to the left of the left hand shift
key

Appendix D

Useful ROM routines

The KERNAL is the operating system of the VIC 20. It contains many subroutines which can be of use to the machine language programmer. All of these can be accessed using a JSR instruction. Control will be returned to your program after the KERNAL subroutine has executed. In the brief descriptions of these subroutines below, the following information is presented.

Name, Purpose
Address : in hex
Communication registers : registers used to pass information to and from the KERNAL subroutine.
Preparatory routines : these routines must be called prior to the subroutine in question.
Possible errors : if an error occurs, when the subroutine returns the carry flag will be set, and the error code will be in the accumulator.
Stack : number of bytes of stack used by the routine.
Registers used : a list of all registers used by the KERNAL routine.

1) Name : ACPTR
   Purpose : Get data from serial bus
   Address : $FFA5
   Communication registers : A; data returned in accumulator
   Prep. routines : TALK, TKSA
   Possible errors : see READST
   Stack : 13
   Registers used : X, A
2) Name : CHKIN
   Purpose : Open a channel for input
   Address : $FFC6
   Communication registers : X; load X with number of logical file to be used
   Prep routines : OPEN
   Possible errors : 3,5,6
   Stack : 0
   Registers used : A,X
3) Name : CHKOUT
   Purpose : Open a channel for output
   Address : $FFC9
   Communication registers : X; load X with logical file number to be used
   Prep. routines : OPEN
   Possible errors : 3,5,7
   Stack : 0
   Registers used : A,X

4) Name : CHRIN
   Purpose : Get a character from input channel
   Address : $FFCF
   Communication registers : A; data byte returned in A
   Prep. routines : OPEN, CHKIN (unless device is keyboard)
   Possible errors : see READST
   Stack : 0
   Registers used : A,X

5) Name : CHROUT
   Purpose : Output a character
   Address : $FFD2
   Communication registers : A; load byte to be output in A
   Prep. routines : OPEN,CHKOUT (unless device is screen)
   Possible errors : see READST
   Stack : 0
   Registers used : A

6) Name : CIOUT
   Purpose : Transmit a byte over the serial bus
   Address : $FFA8
   Communication registers : A; load byte to be output in A
   Prep. routines : LISTEN, (SECOND if device needs secondary
                    address)
   Possible errors : see READST
   Stack : 0
   Registers used : A

7) Name : CLALL
   Purpose : Close all files
   Address : $FFE7
   Communciation registers : none
   Prep. routines : none
   Possible errors : none
   Stack : 11
   Registers used : A,X

8) Name : CLOSE
   Purpose : Close a logical file
   Address $FFC3
   Communication registers : A; load A with logical file number to be
                             closed
   Prep. routines : none
   Possible errors : none
   Stack : 0
   Registers used : A,X

9) Name : CLRCHIN
   Purpose : Clear I/O channels
   Address : $FFCC
   Communication registers : none
   Prep. routines : none

Possible errors : none
Stack : 9
Registers used : A, X

10) Name : GETIN

Purpose : Get a character from keyboard buffer
Address : $FFE4
Communication registers : A; character code returned in A
Prep. routines : none
Possible errors : none
Stack : 0
Registers used : A, X

11) Name : IOBASE

Purpose : Define I/O memory page
Address : $FFF3
Communication registers : X, Y; respectively low and high address bytes of memory section where memory mapped I/O devices are located are returned in X, Y
Prep. routines : none
Possible errors : none
Stack : Two registers used : X, Y

12) Name : LISTEN

Purpose : Command a device on the serial bus to receive data
Address : $FFB1
Communication registers : A; load A with number 4-1, 3 indicating device.
Prep. routines : none
Possible errors : see READST
Stack : 0
Registers used : A

13) Name : LOAD

Purpose : Load RAM from device, or verify
Address : $FFD5
Communication registers : A; set to 0 for load, 1 for verify. X, Y; low and high bytes of starting address of load
Prep. routines : SETLFS, SETNAM
Possible errors : 0,4,5,8,9
Stack : 0
Registers used : A,X,Y

14) Name : MEMBOT

Purpose : Set or read the address of the bottom of RAM
Address : $FF9C
Communication registers : Carry flag; 1 to read, 0 to set bottom of memory. X, Y; low and high bytes of address. If carry is set, the address will be returned in X, Y. If carry clear,

address in X, Y will be transferred to
pointer to bottom of RAM

Prep. routines : none
Possible errors : none
Stack : 0
Registers used : X, Y, P

15) Name: MEMTOP
Purpose : Set or read the address of top of RAM
Address : $FF99
Communication registers : Carry, X, Y; as for MEMBOT
Prep. routines : none
Possible errors : none
Stack : 2
Registers used : X, Y, Carry

16) Name : OPEN
Purpose : Open a logical file
Address : $FFC0
Communication registers : none
Prep. routines : SETLFS, SETNAM
Possible errors : 1,2,4,5,6
Stack : 0
Registers used : A, X, Y

17) Name : PLOT
Purpose : Set cursor location or read cursor location
Address : $FFF0
Communication registers : Carry : 1 for set cursor location
                                          0 for read cursor location
                           X; column number (0-21) returned to or
                               loaded from
                           Y; row number (0-22) returned to or
                               loaded from
Prep. routines : none
Possible errors : none
Stack : 2
Registers used : Carry, X, Y

18) Name : RDTIM
Purpose : Read system clock - 3 byte value
Address : $FFDE
Communication registers : A; most significant byte returned
                          X; next mostsignificant byte returned
                          Y; least significant byte returned
Prep. routines : none
Possible errors : none
Stack : 2
Registers used : A. X. Y

19) Name : READST
Purpose : read status word
Address $FFB7
Communication registers : A; error code returned in A. See discussion of ST in BASIC section for codes and meanings
Prep. routines : none
Possible errors : none
Stack : 2
Registers used : A

20) Name : RESTOR
Purpose : Restore default system and interrupt vectors
Address : $FF8A
Communication registers : none
Prep. routines : none
Possible errors : none
Stack : 2
Registers used : A, X, Y

21) Name : SAVE
Purpose : Save memory to a device
Address : $FFD8
Communication registers : A; load with zero-page address. This address and the next byte contain the address of the start of memory to be saved.
X, Y; low and high bytes of end address of memory to be saved.
Prep. routines : SETLFS, SETNAM (SETNAM not needed if a nameless save to Datasette is desired)
Possible errors : 5,8,9
Stack : 0
Registers used : A, X, Y

22) Name : SCNKEY
Purpose : Scan the keyboard, put value in keyboard queue
Address : $FF9F
Communication registers : none
Prep. routines : none
Possible errors : none
Stack : 0
Registers used : A, X, Y

23) Name : SCREEN
Purpose : Return number of screen rows and columns
Address : $FFED
Communication registers : X; number of columns returned in X
Y; number of rows returned in Y
Prep. routines : none
Possible errors : none

187

Stack : 2
Registers used : X, Y

24) Name : SECOND
Purpose : Send secondary address for LISTEN
Address : $FF93
Communication registers : A; load with secondary address to be
                                            sent
Prep. routines : LISTEN
Possible errors : see READST
Stack : 0
Registers used : A

25) Name : SETLFS
Purpose : Set up a logical file number, device and secondary
addresses
Address : $FFBA
Communication registers : A; load logical file number into A
                                        X; device number
                                        Y; command (secondary address)

Prep. routines : none
Possible errors : none
Stack : 2
Registers used : A, X, Y

26) Name : SETNAM
Purpose : Set up file name
Address : $FFBD
Communication registers : A; load length of file name into A
                                        X, Y; low, high bytes of address of start of
                                        memory where file name is stored

Prep. routines : none
Possible errors : none
Stack : 0
Registers used : A, X, Y

27) Name : SETTIM
Purpose : Set the system clock - 3 byte value
Address : $FFDB
Communication registers : A; most significant byte
                                        X; next most significant byte
                                        Y; least significant byte
Prep. routines : none
Possible errors : none
Stack : 2
Registers used : A, X, Y

28) Name : STOP
Purpose : Check if stop key pressed
Address : $FFE1

Communication registers : zero flag; set if STOP key pressed
Prep. routines : none
Possible errors : none
Stack : 0
Registers used : zero flag, A, X

29) Name : TALK
Purpose : Command a device on the serial bus to TALK
Address : $FFB4
Communication registers : A; load device number into A
Prep. routines : none
Possible errors : see READST
Stack : 0
Registers used : A

30) Name : TKSA
Purpose : send a secondary address to a device commanded to
         TALK
Address : $FF96
Communication registers : A; load secondary address into A
Prep. routines : TALK
Possible errors : see READST
Stack : 0
Registers used : A

31) Name : UNLSN
Purpose : Command all devices on the serial bus to stop receiving
          data
Address : $FFAE
Communication registers : none
Prep. routines : none
Possible errors : see READST
Stack : 0
Registers used : A

32) Name : UNTLK
Puposo : Send an UNTALK command to all devices on serial bus
Address : $FFAB
Communication registers : none
Prep. routines : none
Possible errors : see READST
Stack : 0
Registers used : A

33) Name : VECTOR
Purpose : Set or read system RAM vectors
Address : $FF8D
Communication registers : X, Y; address of list of system RAM
                          vectors
                          Carry flag; if set, the RAM vectors are

read into the list pointed to by X, Y and if clear, the contents of the list pointed to by X, Y are read into the RAM vectors.

Prep. routines : none
Possible errors : none
Stack : 2
Registers used : Carry flag, X, Y

Error Codes

Value	Meaning
0	Routine terminated by STOP key
1	Too many open files
2	File already open
3	File not open
4	File not found
5	Device not present
6	File is not an input file
7	File is not an output file
8	File name is missing
9	Illegal device number

Appendix E

BASIC error messages

BASIC's error messages aren't always illuminating. This list of messages and explanations may be helpful.

BAD DATA:

The program expected numeric data, but received string data (from an OPENed file)

BAD SUBSCRIPT:

The program tried to reference an element of an array whose subscript was outside the dimensions of the array.

CAN'T CONTINUE:

CONT doesn't work because (a) the program was never run, (b) it stopped due to an error condition or (c) an attempt was made to edit the program.

DEVICE NOT PRESENT:

The relevant I/O device isn't present.

DIVISION BY ZERO:

Not allowed.

EXTRA IGNORED:

Too many data items typed in response to an INPUT statement. Only the required numer of items were accepted. Doesn't stop a program.

FILE ALREADY EXISTS:

The name of the source file being copied with the COPY statement alread exists on the destination diskette.

FILE NOT FOUND:

On tape, this means that an END-OF-TAPE marker was found, so search stops. On disk no such file exists.

FILE NOT OPEN:

You tried an I/O command on a file that hasn't been opened.

FILE OPEN:

You tried to open a file using a number assigned to a file already OPEN.

FORMULA TOO COMPLEX:

Either a string expression is too intricate, or an arithmetic expression is too complex. If it's a string, break it up into two parts. If it's an arithmetic expression, try using parentheses.

ILLEGAL DIRECT:

The command attempted in direct mode can only be used in program mode

ILLEGAL QUANTITY:

A number used as an argument is out of range. e.g. POKEing a value greater than 255.

LOAD:

Too many errors (> 31) were found on a tape LOAD

NEXT WITHOUT FOR:
Either you've put in too many NEXT statements, forgotten a FOR statement or branched past a FOR statement.

NOT INPUT FILE:
An attempt has been made to read from a file designated as output only.

NOT OUTPUT FILE:
An attempt has been made to write to a file designated as input only.

OUT OF DATA:
A READ statement has run out of data.

OUT OF MEMORY:
No more RAM left for program or variables. Also caused by too many nested FOR loops and/or GOSUBs. In this case you may have lots of memory but no stack left. You may also have inadvertently changed the top-of-memory pointer.

OVERFLOW:
The result of a calculation is greater than 1.70141884E+38.

REDIM'D ARRAY:
An array name appears in more than one DIM statement, or has been both implicitly and explicitly DIMensioned.

REDO FROM START:
An INPUT statement received the wrong type of data. Doesn't stop the program, just continues prompting until the correct type of data is input.

RETURN WITHOUT GOSUB:
A RETURN for which there is no corresponding GOSUB. Usually caused by dropping into the subroutine inadvertently.

STRING TOO LONG:
Strings can be a maximum of 255 characters long.

SYNTAX:
BASIC doesn't recognise the statement.

TYPE MISMATCH:
Number used in place of string, or vice-versa.

UNDEF'D FUNCTION:
A user defined function was called but has not yet been defined, with a DEF FN statement

UNDEF'D STATEMENT:
An attempt has been made to go to a non-existent line number.

VERIFY:
The program on tape or disk being VERIFYd does not match the program in memory.

Current Key Pressed

Location 197 stores a coded value of the current key depressed. If more than one key is depressed the higher value is stored.

Key	Value	Key	Value	Key	Value	Key	Value
1	0	none	16	SPACE	32	Q	48
3	1	A	17	Z	33	E	49
5	2	D	18	C	34	T	50
7	3	G	19	B	35	U	51
9	4	J	20	M	36	O	52
+	5	L	21	•	37	@	53
£	6	;	22	none	38	↑	54
DEL	7	CRSR ⇆	23	f1	39	f5	55
←	8	STOP	24	none	40	2	56
W	9	none	25	S	41	4	57
R	10	X	26	F	42	6	58
Y	11	V	27	H	43	8	59
I	12	N	28	K	44	0	60
P	13	,	29	:	45	—	61
*	14	/	30	=	46	HOME	62
RETURN	15	CRSR ↕	31	f3	47	f7	63

INDEX

Mastering the Commodore 64

Mark Greenshields

www.ingramcontent.com/pod-product-compliance
Lightning Source LLC
LaVergne TN
LVHW041204050326
832903LV00020B/450